YOUR CHILD CAN BE
TOP
OF THE CLASS

A parents' guide

NEW EDITION

KEN ADAMS

MICHAEL O'MARA BOOKS LIMITED

First published in Great Britain in 1991
by Michael O'Mara Books Limited,
9 Lion Yard, Tremadoc Road, London SW4 7NQ

Revised Edition 1997

A CIP catalogue record for this book is available from the
British Library.

ISBN 1-85479-243-1

Designed by Mick Keates

Printed and bound in England by Clays Ltd, St Ives plc

CONTENTS

CHAPTER ONE

INTRODUCTION

'Can you help my 6-year-old son?' asked the mother. 'He's very slow at school.' I helped him, for half-an-hour a week, and left a small amount of work for his mother to give him each day. A year later, this boy who had been bottom of his class was top. In Maths, in particular, he was a whiz kid. This is most certainly not an isolated case. Where parents have the know-how and have encouraged their child at home, schoolwork has improved dramatically.

The reasons for such an improvement are several: One-to-one tutoring is an infinitely more efficient method of teaching than class teaching. A tutor can tailor the work to the needs of the child, he is in a perfect position to bolster confidence and he can smooth out any problems that the child has with the work then and there. A close relationship is built up between tutor and pupil that cannot be developed in a classroom situation. It is this relationship that can lead the tutor to tap into the hidden potential of a child. For example, an exceptional pupil can labour for years in a middle set in school because, for one reason or another, she has become adept at fooling her teacher. She has found, perhaps that if she claims she cannot do something she is given easier work and as time goes on begins to believe that she is not as 'clever' as some of her classmates. An astute parent tutor will be able to spot such behaviour and walk the delicate tight-rope between knowing that a child truly does not understand how to do something and believing that he can, if his unused potential is tapped.

In solving a problem many skills must be brought to bear by a child. Initially, she must be able to understand what certain symbols mean, whether they be mathematical or language based and must be able to communicate in like language in return. In between, particular facets of intelligence are used in solving the core of the problem. Many children, it appears, do not lack the ability to perform the latter. It is in the first area, an area that might be termed one of communication skills, that the child seems to be lacking. She cannot do the problem, for example, because she does not properly understand the meaning of a word or the meaning of the subtleties of the construction of a sentence.

The failure of many schools to press ahead effectively with the teaching of traditional learning skills like reading, spelling, punctuation, table learning, word knowledge and sentence construction, means that these skills, and others, taught over a period of time at home, will considerably improve the child's over-all performance. It will appear to the teacher that the child's basic intelligence has, for some strange reason, increased markedly, whereas she has simply developed the effective communication skills in Mathematics and Language.

A parent is more likely to believe in a hidden and untapped potential in her child than anyone else. She wishes it to be so, and it therefore is so, because her belief and confidence transmits to the child who unwittingly taps into his latent potential. This belief by a parent or tutor in a child's ability is the single most important factor in improving a child's performance in schoolwork. A parent tutor 'trains' the child's confidence and belief in himself. So many times I was told that something was 'impossible' for that child to do, or 'that'll be the day' that she does that. In the end I found that I had myself underestimated what the child could do. Many others underestimate out of sight and their disbelief makes the possible impossible. In actual fact, the mind is highly malleable and the dominant factors in learning are time and method, not intelligence.

The high priority laid by schools on a child being happy can greatly hinder her progress and lead to her becoming bored. It is, of course, essential that a relaxed atmosphere is developed in association with learning but happiness for a child may be a football match, a horse ride, cartoons on television, a strawberry ice-cream or a cuddle from mum, and not a division sum. Much learning is bound to be irksome at some stage, however well presented, and it is no reflection on the teacher's ability if a child is finding his work boring. The mistake of educators is to downgrade the standard of work, or even to throw out whole chunks of the Syllabus, in the mistaken assumption that this will make things more palatable and stimulate interest. It is more likely to lead to under-achievement. Attempts to make all learning interest-based has, in many instances, led to a watering down of academic rigour. While no fair-minded person would support the punishing rigours of past education systems, the other extreme of pandering to the very elusive and volatile whims of young children, and especially teenagers, is doomed to failure. There is also the question of whether the motivating interest should be of long-term or short-term worth. At home, a parent is better placed to explain long-term worth when there is no sudden rush of interest in the subject to hand. Monotonous and repetitive work, in particular, is best done under the perceived fair-minded hand of a parent.

In school, many teachers categorise children from early on – they are bright, average or below average. It is easier to organise a class on this basis. Unfortunately, this leads a child to perform within the particular category in which he is placed and because a top group learns more than a bottom group, a child will find it difficult to catch up at some later date. So, categorisation in the Infant School tends to more or less permanent categorisation throughout the entire school system. Many never recover from this, and it is often difficult to get a child re-categorised, even when they have done extra work at home. It is only when a test or exam result shows significant improvement that a teacher can be persuaded that a child should be moved up to a higher group or set.

At home, of course, there are none of these difficulties over the 'setting' or 'grouping' of children. A parent can simply work, with no preconceptions, to get the best out of her child.

Many teaching methods are the result of imposed ideals from above in the education system – from educationists in University and advisors in local authorities. They are essentially experimental because the result of such methods take years to assess and even the conclusions on the worth of such methods are certainly not clear-cut. Some, of course, represent genuine advances in educational thinking which have valuable practical applications, but others are simply fads upon which ambitious educationists, eager to be seen as up-to-date, have thrown themselves with gusto and total disregard for the real needs of the child. The teaching of reading, in particular, has suffered from more than its fair share of disastrous innovation, including the Initial Teaching Alphabet (I.T.A.) phonic method, which ruined the spelling ability of a whole generation, and the modern 'Real Books' method which threatens to delay the onset of many a child's reading by a decade or two. Another interesting novelty in Primary Schools recently has been an attempt to invite stories from children who know nothing about beginnings, middles and endings and who certainly do not have the simplest pre-requisite skills of spelling, punctuation and sentence construction.

At home a parent tutor does not have to operate within the restrictions of these impositions from above. He or she is free to find the most effective way to teach her child, but should not necessarily expect to be advised by educationists. Many parents of successful children who have used rather old, but tried and tested methods at home, have found that the educational establishment does not take kindly to having its prized methods held up to ridicule. Too many people and too many vested interests are at stake. Many a career in education hangs on the success or failure of a new Reading System or Reading Series.

There are, of course, many sound ideas operating in schools which should not be ignored by parents. Learning by discovery is very valuable. However, it is impossible to teach everything by discovery. This type of learning takes time. A parent teaching at home may employ some discovery, but reception learning methods are quicker. It is often easier and more effective for a parent simply to inform her child.

This is not to say that many things should not be taught practically at home. For example, counting and division are taught best using counters or buttons: children learn many method concepts best through concrete associations and it is particularly easy for a parent to organise this type of learning in the home. In school, where class numbers are large, there are severe organisational difficulties in making certain aspects of learning concrete and meaningful.

For the above reasons, a parent teaching traditional skills with some problem solving at home will greatly enhance their child's school performance. No teacher is immune to a child who reads well, writes well, does mechanical arithmetic well and can solve problems to an above average extent so he will be perceived as being more intelligent as well. All skills can be taught at home by a parent working with her child for under half-an-hour a day. Whatever the initial standard of attainment, the child is bound to improve and sometimes to a startling extent.

Some schools, of course, are better than others at drawing out the inner capabilities of the child. Others manage to be very effective in teaching communication skills. Parent tutors are in the happy position of being able to be effective in all aspects of teaching. Where whole communities embark on home education the children benefit in school accordingly. Reports in the U.S.A. and in the U.K. have shown that Asian pupils do best at school. They spend more money on tutors and more on home learning materials than other communities. One Asian community I know of not only has most of its children tutored in Arabic and other Moslem related subjects, but also in English and Maths. In spite of obvious language difficulties, many Asian families are stunningly successful academically.

Areas of home education
Experience teaches that the areas of help most needed to improve your child's performance at school are:

In English
(1) Reading
(2) Constructing simple sentences
(3) Spelling
(4) Writing a simple, interesting story
(5) Comprehension
(6) Word knowledge
(7) Clear handwriting
(8) Punctuation

In Maths
(1) Counting and knowing the names of numbers
(2) 'Carrying' in both addition and subtraction
(3) Division
(4) Simple, worded problems
(5) Telling the time
(6) Converting metric units
(7) Shopping sums
(8) Fractions and simple ratio
(9) Decimals in general

If a child in his final year at primary school is competent in all the above he has a good chance of being top of the class. Most children, however, fall down in one or many of the above skills.

The earlier the child is caught in its progress through the school system, the better the chance of success. A parent can certainly ensure, as many are doing, that their child stays at the top of the class if home education is begun at the age of 5 or 6.

Saturation learning
Maths is a difficult subject for school children. Topics are taught so that each builds on a previously learnt and related topic: learning is structured and divided in stages or steps. This means that if one step is forgotten, a whole house of cards built on that step is in danger of collapse. A tutor must therefore ensure that each previous step is fully understood before a new one is taught. Unfortunately, a step often has a uniqueness of its own and children can forget the mechanism within that step if consolidation is not effected regularly. Certain subtraction sums with borrowing are prime examples. If the sums are not practised consistently over the years a child will forget. She will then have to relearn at a later stage, with consequent loss of confidence. Sometimes there will be failure in a test or exam, reinforcing the idea that she is no good at Maths.

The solution is to practise not only recently learnt skills but also those previously learnt which are not yet incorporated into long-term memory. This may mean retaining practice of the Two Times table when a child is learning the Three Times, Four Times and even Five Times table. She is constantly returning to an earlier step to consolidate, walking up three steps and stepping back two. Only when a step is known so thoroughly that a child can perform the skill while standing on her head should its revision be abandoned. Saturation has been achieved through 'overlearning'. This means that a long list of steps to be revised will be built up as the learner progresses and from time to time the bottom steps will be lopped off. This avoids a situation that frequently arises in Secondary Schools where subjects are learnt in rapid succession throughout the year. By the time subject number ten has been learnt, subject number one has been all but forgotten. Rarely does a syllabus allow for frequent revision of earlier skills as suggested by the technique of saturation learning.

The following chapters give advice on helping a child at various stages of her education. The earlier a parent begins with such help, the greater is the advantage she gives to her child. Starting with a child who has newly entered school ensures that he or she is always in a top group or is at least thought of by a teacher as being one of the bright ones.

Many teachers believe that intelligence 'will out' and that it is the natural order of things that a slow pupil will fall to the bottom of the class. This is not so. I have helped many children to stay at the top of the class through home education. Some most certainly were bright but others were of average intelligence and ability. Even slow pupils managed to hold their own at a level above the median.

Finally, a parent who shows persistence in setting aside short learning periods for her child and impresses her with a sense of the long-term worth of education, will see her grow in confidence and also express satisfaction in the completion of a task well done.

CHAPTER TWO

HOW CHILDREN LEARN

'I'm trying to make the picture,' said the small boy. I was about to explain to him how to solve the simple problem that I had set because for about three minutes now he had been staring vacantly at the words in front of him. 'I know how to do it,' he continued. 'I made the picture.' Time and again, I have had to wait while a child has read an example and then looked away to stare at some imaginary point in space. Each time he was trying to link the information given with something in his memory. Students of Applied Mathematics do the same when they try to visualise the resolution of forces. Only then can they understand and complete the problem.

Creating a mental image whether of a sound, a shape, a word or a concept, and trying to match and link it with something in memory is a prerequisite to understanding. The establishment of the link between the item of information and memory confers meaning on that item.

There are levels of meaning, however. A child sitting in a classroom listening to a teacher reading a story may allow his attention to wander. He hears the word sounds and recognises that it is English but at the end of the story cannot repeat the content. He has failed to link the images he has formed in his mind of words to items in memory that confer deeper meaning. He has linked only to the sound of the words and to something that tells him that the language is English. However, this information still has meaning, although at a more superficial level.

Memory structure

How the mind processes information, how we establish information in memory and how we think is the subject of some debate. Central to this debate is the memory process which in simplified form may be considered to consist of a sensory memory, short-term memory and long-term memory. Sensory memory accepts input messages in coded form through the sense organs and holds it for only a very short time, producing an image that lingers for a time. The coded information of the outside world is then passed on to short-term memory, which holds it for longer. This creates a mental image of the information and initiates a search of long-term memory for a 'matching' or near-matching coded mental image. Concentration and the content of the information will determine whether the search is at a superficial level or at a deeper one.

When the 'match' is made between the mental image of the incoming material and the image created from long-term memory, a link is cemented (although it is initially a tenuous one) and meaning is conferred.

Long-term memory is a vast network of established memories in the form of linked coded plans or schemata, similar to a filing system that is constantly being added to, reviewed and edited. The major period for reassortment of linkages is probably in sleep.

When a new link has been made with long-term memory it is usually necessary to repeat the input soon after different input material has displaced it from short-term memory. Much repetition of similar material, or practice, far beyond the point where it has been understood and memorised is called overlearning, and establishes the material in long-term memory. (*See* overleaf.)

For the young child, it is essential that early learning should be related to real life either by using real-life objects or pictures. The sudden change, when starting school, from real-life learning to abstract learning, in the shape of the printed word and

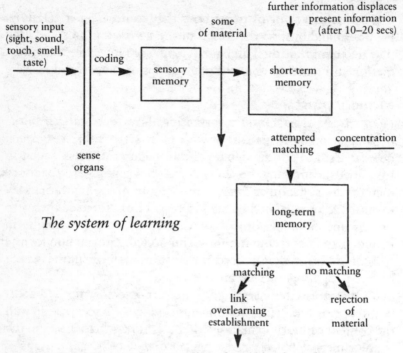

The system of learning

numbers, needs to be continually referred back to the concrete to create a match of mental images and effect meaning.

The system of learning consists theoretically of an *input* through the sense organs, *processing* within the central nervous system, and an *output*, which is our response in learning, or the writing of reports, the practising of skills and so on. The central phase of learning, that within the central nervous system itself, is crucial because it determines both how material should be presented to a learner and what a child should do to consolidate material in long-term memory.

Real-life learning

Learning from and about real life begins at birth and even before a baby is born. It results in an established network of coded meanings for what we have encountered in our lives.

We do not need to practise or overlearn consciously to establish information from real life in memory. This is partly because of the concrete nature of life and the clear mental image it creates and because overlearning is inbuilt into real-life experience. It is also because linkage takes place within a highly established network of experience and so learning is relatively swift and highly efficient.

If I go to a new town and walk down a strange street, the next day I can remember clearly many aspects of my walk. A certain amount of overlearning has occurred because I scan the street continually as I walk down it and the experience concentrates my attention for a continuous period of time. The mental image of that street will also be linked to that of a typical street. Nobody had to tell me that it was a street because I understood that. The meaning of the new street has been incorporated into memory by some linking and modification of the typical model. Even if I had never seen a street before I would still be able to link the mental image of that street with *something* in long-term memory, such as recognition of depth, colour, height and form. I still achieve a sense of understanding, although not of the deeper meaning of the concept of a street.

Furthermore, the mental image of this new street, now incorporated into long-term memory, is also linked to another well established network in memory and that is one that relates to the passage of time. By referring to a certain time on that day, I can determine where I was.

Concepts

The concept of a street is built upon the concepts of pavement, building, lamp-post and other subsidiary concepts. Without having the meanings of those concepts incorporated into memory I could not comprehend the deeper meaning of 'street'. In learning, there is often a hierarchy of concepts and an understanding of one may depend on other prerequisite concepts. Certain areas of Mathematics are structured in this way: a child cannot understand addition at the deeper level until he understands number. There would simply be nothing in long-term memory to link to. It is possible, of course, to learn by rote or to substitute rules for understanding. However, failing to learn concepts will result in gaps in understanding that will hinder progress. Learning tables for example, involves understanding at a low level. The use of tables is certainly helpful in speeding division and the equivalence of fractions calculations but the underlying meaning of multiplication must not be lost. Later areas of Mathematics will have to be linked to this deeper meaning.

Schoolwork

Real-life experience is a continuous phenomenon. We are constantly exercising the wires that connect real life to memory. Schoolwork is different. It never results in a continual usage of our sensory equipment. A child of 5 may spend half-an-hour a day learning to read although much of that time will not be concentrating on subject matter. At the same time the child is using most of his senses for every waking minute perfecting his sense of balance and direction. The fact that very young children learn by a great deal of overlearning, including the establishing of an extensive network for spoken language and gesture, suggests that learning can be greatly enhanced by clear presentation of input. This means an involvement of as many of the senses as possible, by the focusing of attention and by repetition. Learning is certainly not merely a function governed by the age of a person. Meanings, including deeper meanings, can be learnt at an early age if the prerequisite skills are there.

Speed of learning

All of us would recognise that some children learn quicker than others. The reasons for this could be many. In terms of the Information Processing model of learning presented here failure to learn may be at three points:

(1) at input, presented material may be unclear or there may be environmental distractions to learning.
(2) in processing, there may be some deficiency in the sensory apparatus (in hearing or sight, for example) and this will lead to incorrect coding of material.
(3) in short-term memory, one child may take longer to match a mental image of information with that in long-term memory and another child may have more extensive memory networks. The child whose memory does not have the schemata to link to given information is at an inappropriate stage of development.

The factors that lead to concentration, which is the effective force that drives new information to link into memory, can be positive or negative. Positive factors could be the fostering of natural curiosity (as in discovery methods with some objectives), the desire to please others (especially parents), the competitive instinct, a certain amount of anxiety which is related to a desire to succeed, success and praise, giving goals (even if it is only the thought of a break for a drink), rewards, and the inherent interest of the subject matter. Negative factors include physical and mental tiredness, great anxiety, too much failure and criticism, discovery without clear objectives (leading to boredom), a bad learning environment (too much noise or, sometimes, too much quiet), and dull subject matter.

Finally, to consolidate material into long-term memory there must be an output of material. This includes practice, which effects overlearning and establishes particular information and also writing about the experience to be learned and talking about it, which results in links with other schemata, or information, in memory.

Recall and forgetting

Placing information into long-term memory is one thing, recalling it or preventing it from being forgotten is another. In spite of all that we do to ensure that understanding is achieved, some information still gets lost. Either it is unavailable for recall because it is tucked away in some dark recess of memory where the lines of communication are not often opened, it is repressed or it decays. Sometimes, we think that something has been incorporated into long-term memory, when it has been displaced from short-term memory by other incoming material before there is time for matching. Another likelihood is that the distinctive nature of a particular schema has become blurred with the passing of time and has merged into the general structure of the schema to which it is linked. If I do not visit a street for some years the recollection of it becomes more and more hazy as it approximates to the more generalised picture that I have of a street. When I return for a visit I find an impostor to the vision that I held in memory.

CHAPTER THREE

HOW CAN I HELP MY CHILD TO LEARN?

The struggle to match sensory input with established schemata in long-term memory is the attempt to create a completed mental image. The completion of this link is the essence of understanding and overlearning establishes the information in memory. Every link in the network chain represents an additional facet of understanding. The thrill of teaching a child is in reducing knowledge to a form that will create a mental image which will link easily to what you know is in his memory. It is a matching and linking of the information that you present to the meaning of something closely related in his memory that creates new meaning or confirms it.

Real-life meaning

For human beings sight is the dominant sense but the effect of the other senses should not be neglected, as they produce mental images too. The bark of a dog will immediately invoke the image of a dog (unless you have never seen one before) and all that 'dog' means. A 5-year-old who is learning to read 'dog' will most likely have the deeper understanding or concept of 'dog' in memory. Showing her a picture of a dog reinforces the image. Writing the word 'dog' beneath the picture of a dog and saying the word while tracing out the letter shapes makes it relatively easy to learn. The word 'dog', however, represents a concrete concept. 'Mercy' on the other hand is abstract. It is more difficult to create a mental image of 'mercy' and therefore its meaning often escapes young children, even though they may learn to read it by recognising its shape and sound. To invoke a mental image of 'mercy' and give it meaning in a deeper sense it is necessary to draw a picture. Every time I hear the word 'mercy', I have a very brief glimpse of a man on his knees wringing his hands and begging to an unseen tormentor. The picture tells a story and telling stories with words and pictures is a powerful way of teaching difficult concepts. Acting out the meaning of the word provides further consolidation.

'The' and 'a' are usually learned initially in reading by their shape and sound alone. They are more difficult for a child to visualise in terms of deeper meaning (for example, bring me *the*, definite, book about gardening, as opposed to *a* book to read). Continual practice through real-life experience is necessary and this is why children of ethnic minorities have great difficulty with word meanings. These children simply do not have enough practice with English words when the main language spoken at home (and often among friends in the playground, too) is Urdu or Gujerati.

Of course, it is not always possible to provide concrete objects in order to teach something. You cannot for example bring a monkey from the zoo every time you wish to reinforce the concept of 'monkey' and teach a child to learn to read it with deeper meaning. You can however, provide a picture of a monkey and you can, if you are so inclined, act out the part of one (this might be very instructive, as the sight and sound of a parent attempting to be a monkey could be very memorable). Furthermore, bizarre images seem to be remembered best. To a small child a monkey looks like a grizzled version of his father and the word 'monkey' itself seems to have an interesting shape. Perhaps this is why 'monkey' was the first word my son learnt to read when he was only 10 months old, after being shown a picture in a book in association with the word, and later saying 'monkey' with the picture covered. The sight of such a creature, even in a book, captured his imagination and linked the sound and shape of the associated word in his memory.

Using all the senses

Learning through real-life experience is very effective because there is overlearning through using many of the senses and providing links in memory. Sometimes it is possible to provide a link to real life by visualising it and linking items in this way. To teach your child to read a word like 'chair' for example, you can draw a picture of it, label a real chair, get her to trace the word in a sand tray, write it, or tell her to close her eyes and visualise a chair with the word below. You can emphasise the sound of the word and its shape (**h** looks like a chair).

There are further techniques that are perhaps more applicable to a slightly older child. Items of knowledge that cannot be easily related to real life can be visualised as being linked to, sitting on or behind, something familiar in real life (a favourite toy or ornament, for example). A story form coupled with visualisation is useful for sequences: 'I have my breakfast and put *1* on the table, I eat my dinner and put *2* in the custard . . .' Again, bizarre and humorous incidents focus the concentration and produce very clear mental images. The rhyme '1, 2 . . . buckle my shoe . . .' also provides an additional link between similar sounds, and rhymes and sing-song methods of teaching sequences are very effective (singing the alphabet for example).

Numbers can be learnt by 'chunking'. A long number is broken down into smaller units, learnt separately, and then joined together by visualisation. Similarly, problems can be broken down into their essential operations and the links and sequence of a solution represented diagramatically. In this way, a wide variety of strategies for the solutions of problems can be taught and are very applicable to the teaching of Maths.

Presentation

In order to create a link with memory, clear speaking, pausing to allow time for matching to occur, repeating sounds, drawing simple pictures, and questioning your child about the subject matter, can provide that vital link with memory and contribute to overlearning. Clearness of presentation is important and is illustrated by the following incident. I had just lost my spectacles, blown off in a storm and now lying somewhere in Greater Manchester. As I walked along the road, I was surprised to see on the opposite side four very tall soldiers in white uniforms with black peaked hats, standing stiff and erect to attention. Apprehensively, I approached, only to find that the vision disappeared and was replaced by four white-washed gateposts at the entrance to neighbouring houses. The blurred image had linked to an entirely inappropriate section of memory.

You must ensure that the information you present to a child accurately creates the image that you want it to. Furthermore, the language that you use to explain something to a child must be appropriate. Often a child either misinterprets what you are saying or does not understand at all.

'I do not understand,' says the child. I explain the problem fully to her again, being careful to leave scope for her to link concepts in her mind (telling her the answer leads her to learn a process, which has superficial meaning).

'Oh,' she says, 'I didn't understand that word.' She points to one particular word.

Sometimes, children think they understand a word but attach to it an entirely different meaning from the adult meaning. Working with very young children over many years it has become glaringly obvious to me that words like 'more' and 'the same', for example, are often used to refer to height or distance and not to amount or quantity.

The material you present to a child must also be appropriate to his level of learning: diagrams are generally not understood by infant children, whereas real-life (practical) experiences are.

Interference

For many early readers the **b** and **d** *sounds* are often confused and as much as possible these sounds should be separated in the learning of letter sounds. Visualisation techniques applied to the letters seem to work well. Both images are facing to the right which is the direction in which a child reads.

b is a boot   **d** is a duck

Similar *shapes* also cause interference. For instance, **n** and **h** look alike but enlarging the letters emphasises the difference.

Ruth has been having difficulty distinguishing vowel sounds: **e** sounds like **i** and she sometimes has trouble sorting out the other vowel sounds even though, at 6, she reads very well.

A mediating link works well in this instance. Thus:

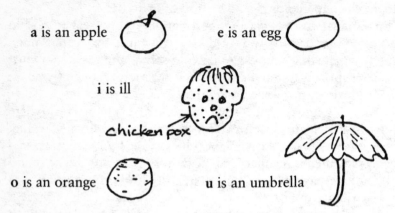

a is an apple   **e** is an egg

i is ill

chicken pox

o is an orange   **u** is an umbrella

Other distractions can result when previously learnt material interferes with that being learnt at present, or when something being learnt now interferes with that learnt some time ago. 'Cramming' information can result in ineffective learning for these reasons. Reading along with a child can also result in slow learning of words because of interruptions.

Emphasising distinctive characteristics followed by overlearning can prevent forgetting. The Look and Say method of learning words emphasises their distinctive shapes and effects overlearning by the use of flash cards. Use of a Key Words scheme also facilitates quick success in reading by emphasising words which are used most in reading texts. This gives children confidence when they find that they learn to read quickly and it more than compensates for the stilted nature of the text.

Discovery learning

This method allows a child to find out for herself about her world. Without giving a child some objectives, discovery learning tends to lead to boredom and there is certainly no concrete proof that discovery teaches better than reception learning, where a parent or teacher tells a child the answer. When the time involved in discovery is taken into account reception learning scores heavily. Discovery, however, does take account of the natural curiosity of children and certainly links between schemata in long-term memory will be made that otherwise would not. In the search for an answer through discovery a child is learning how to employ strategies as she works out things from first principles. A parent who teaches her child would be best advised to include some discovery learning from time to time. Science in the home is a very convenient subject with which to introduce this. Even extremely young children, for example, can learn about flotation when playing with objects in the bath. Your child should always be encouraged to ask 'Why?'.

Saturation learning and overlearning

The four great rules of learning are understanding first, followed by practice, practice and even more practice. This might sound like a demand for more sing-song repetition of tables but it is not. As I have indicated, overlearning can be effected in a variety of interesting and meaningful ways. Saturation learning, for example, is the retention of an apparently well-learnt and understood subject on a weekly revision list with new work. In this way, the overlearning is a steady process and is hardly noticed by a child.

Incentives and disincentives to learning

Motivation is a powerful ally in the armoury of weapons used to develop concentration and cement that vital link between coded information from the world and memory, hopefully resulting in deep meaning.

There should, of course, ideally be no distractions when children learn but in practice there are many. The television may be a distraction if a favourite programme is on but the absence of the familiar hum of the television may also be a distraction. Some children who grow up in a busy household are distracted by silence. It will be necessary for you to discover for yourself in what environment your child works best.

The attention span for different ages is important. One to two minutes for every year of life is a rule-of-thumb guide, which means approximately 15–20 minutes for an 11-year-old before a short break. However, I find that this varies from child to child: John could concentrate well for 20 minutes as a 2-year-old, whereas some 16-year-olds find 10 minutes unbearable.

You should encourage your child to provide himself with realistic work targets. You can provide rewards to give him something to look forward to – a television programme or a break with a drink and biscuit.

A considerable disincentive to learning is tiredness. Strenuous physical exercise leaves its mark for some time, reducing concentration dramatically: Carol played school badminton on Tuesday and three hours later her ability to apply herself to her favourite subjects was still very low.

Emotional factors that can affect concentration were detailed in the last chapter but a special mention should be made of the use of humour in developing a conducive atmosphere to learning. One minute of laughter, it is said, can relax a person for up to 45 minutes. It does not seem to prevent the mild anxiety which is a motivating factor but rather reduces over-anxiety and the resulting tension.

It helps if the subject matter itself is humorous. One of the reasons for the success of Roald Dahl's stories is the quirky humour involved. I have tried out the Samson Superslug letters, used here for spelling practice, on many children and the humour makes for very relaxed learning times.

Another way to introduce humour and assist concentration, is to state that every mistake a child makes is going to cost him £100, and then soberly add up what he owes you at the end of learning time (one boy ended up owing me £47,000 at £1,000 per mistake!).

Concepts and problem solving

When teaching children new concepts you will need to develop the idea of the concept in general before teaching in detail. For instance, knowledge of a wide variety of trees and their common characteristics will establish the meaning of 'tree'. This in turn establishes in memory a schema onto which the modifications imparted by the characteristics of specific trees can be grafted.

Before learning a new concept, old concepts on which it relies should be revised. When starting to learn percentages, for example, it will be helpful for the child to revise multiplication, division, the equivalence of fractions and also the meaning of 'one whole'.

Problem solving and investigations are more complex. You will need to break problems down so that your child can see how concepts or processes are linked. A problem like 'What two numbers add up to 28, but subtract to make 6?' is a monstrous trial for a child below the age of about 11. Adults find it easy because they have met this sort of problem in everyday life for years when shopping, and have the number bonds, or links in long-term memory, that tell them: $11 + 17 = 28$ and $17 - 11 = 6$.

If your child is able to encounter a wide variety of problems set in verbal, mathematical and practical contexts, she will learn to search within her memory for links that can be made between schemata. The intellectual effort of drawing together wide-ranging concepts through a scientific or mathematical investigation so that a link can be obtained, will itself be stored in long-term memory. In other words, a child, through practice, remembers strategies and these are a reminder that the search for links between schemata is not merely a passive thing. Just as writing a story is creative, so is an investigation. In Mathematics in particular, children need to learn that there is not always a set answer to a problem and also to develop confidence in their own abilities. A fixed attitude in children to problem solving is a considerable hindrance to progress in this area and they should be encouraged to approach a problem by weighing up the alternatives.

Grouping material

It is important to seek patterns in Mathematics and some of these links are very useful in real life. For example, if I wish to change 2 tens for twos, then I instantly know that I will get ten twos: $2 \times 10 = 10 \times 2$. This pattern is not obvious to all children up to the age of 11, something which amazes most parents.

Systems for input speed up the learning process because this seems to be the way that memory links items together. The grouping and ordering of material works particularly well with slow learners and very young children. Isolating vowel sounds in the initial stages of learning spelling helps some learners: bat, mat, cat, hat, sat, rat, fat. This group of words also puts together similar shapes. Linking such words effects easier recall and overlearning by a multisensory approach.

Output

Output is the use of creative writing, reports, discussions, model building, painting, scrapbooks, practice examples and other methods to cement new information in memory and to develop links between schemata. Some of these links should be between schemata that have deeper meaning. There is always a danger that your child will think and work at a superficial level. It is possible, for example, to learn a large amount of Maths by linking processes in your mind.

$$\begin{array}{r} 23\ '4 \\ -\ 1\ 9 \\ \hline 1\ 5 \end{array}$$

The above is a process and learnt as such will have only super-ficial meaning. It is essential, therefore, that from time to time you refer your child back to the fact that 34 is 3 tens and 4 units and that you have borrowed 1 ten. (*See* page 52 for more on Tens and Units.)

In everyday life we communicate generally at the superficial level 'skimming' each other's conversations and our own thoughts for meanings. In the learning situation, your child should be encouraged to look for *deeper* meanings in words, in Mathematics and in other areas. Only then can she truly fulfil her potential.

Pre-school learning at home

Before dealing with the school child it is worth mentioning a little about the pre-school child who may or may not go to a nursery school. At this age children learn best through play and certainly through concrete activities such as handling objects when learning. Language is best learnt through conversation with adults and older children and by learning the names of household objects and the deeper meaning of words. This means that a parent tutor will need to approach consciously the teach-ing of her child. The early activities in the next chapter intended primarily for infant children, are particularly appropriate for bright 3- and 4-year-olds. Even some 2-year-olds (and younger) can be taught to read. Two of my children were taught to read before the age of 2 and have never looked back. The impetus of their early learning experience, if consistently built upon, will result in a lively, confident and perceptive mind.

CHAPTER FOUR

YOUR CHILD FROM FIVE TO SEVEN

A 5-year-old likes to talk. In fact, some talk incessantly. They have an interest in using new and large words, they ask questions and search for information. Their grammar is reasonably accurate, apart from the ethnic minority children. They love to be read to and hopefully this has occurred from an early age. Young children love rhymes, jingles and fairy stories. However, they do muddle concepts: if told for example, that two female cats are white and two male cats are black, they will often assume that all female cats are white and all male cats are black.

A 5-year-old can also name some of the days of the week and knows several colours. He is also aware of the concept of month, season, yesterday and tomorrow and can usually answer the question, 'What day is it?' He also loves cartoons on the television, especially the Walt Disney ones.

By 7 years of age many a child has learnt to use language complainingly and also uses slang and clichés. He can detail the similarities and differences between two objects. A 7-year-old can tell the time and know what time he goes to school. He is interested in cooking, keeping house, pets, animals, holidays, the latest television cartoon series and books. He can distinguish left from right and he has developed a deepening sense of meanings and relationships, and can make comments about the behaviour of characters in television soap operas.

The above, of course, is an 'average' child of these ages. In reality, there are many differing behaviour patterns at the same age. Philip, at 6, reads very well and can tackle a wide range of sums. He is very confident; he tells me what he wants to be taught and his suggestions are very sensible. Sonia, at the same age, says very little and although she loves the learning times, she is at an early stage of reading and talks using only one or two words at a time. Carol who is also 6, reads and converses well and has a quick wit. Although all three recognise the humour in what I say (usually exaggeration) Carol always comes back with a witty rejoinder: 'I'm much quicker than you.' I say: 'I could easily read that whole book in two seconds.' Immediately, handing me the book she says 'Let's see you do it, then.' (Her parents sitting nearby collapsed in laughter.)

In general, 5-year-olds seem to be happy and well adjusted but by 7 they have often become much more withdrawn.

ENGLISH: READING

Formal reading instruction is at the heart of the education of the infant school child. Two of the earliest and best methods of instruction – phonics and the whole word (Look and Say) method – are still used today. An integrated language scheme is advocated in Britain, similar to that used in the U.S.A. This involves labelling real-life objects and pictures with single words, tracing letters in sand-trays, learning key words (words that occur most frequently in text), phonics, learning the alphabet, look and say, reading stories along with your child, writing and discussing subjects.

Pre-reading

Read to your child whenever possible, especially rhymes, fairy stories and jingles. As you read, trace your finger over the words, from left to right. Put labels on familiar objects, including toys. Use script letters:

a b c d e f g h i j k l m n o p q r s t u v w x y z

Reading cards

Draw or paste a picture on white card. Above or beneath the picture write the word in large clear letters. Sit down with your child sometime in the day for 10 minutes and go through the cards reading the words out loud and talking about the pictures. Use about 5 or 6 cards at any one time. There are many books that present words and pictures well. They are usually in the A-B-C book section in book shops.

After a week of showing a few cards or picture-book words to your child, you can try covering up the picture and asking him to say the word. If he cannot, simply uncover the picture and continue. It may take longer for him really to 'read' the word.

List of words to pair with a picture

apple   man   dog   cat   lion   monkey   tiger
elephant   house   garden   flower   grass   book
bed   newspaper   aeroplane   orange   banana   tree
horse (do not include with house)   baby   table   chair
letter   spoon   dish   football   parrot   hat   bus
cake   shop   window   shoes   socks   knife   postman
milkman   door   carpet   hand   foot   arm   leg
gloves   dress   lorry   train   doll   teddy   bread
sweet   lamp-post   school   coat   library   cooker
television   fork   fire   bicycle   road   pavement   cup
lady   grandma   grandad

Don't worry about repeating the same words and pictures many times over for a number of weeks. Children tire far less quickly of repetition than you will.

Look and Say

This is a method that relies on your child recognising the shape of a word. When you have read through a book with him (select a title from the list at the end of this section) make a few 'flash cards' by writing some words clearly on card. Make a game of showing the word to your child, ask him to trace out the shape of the letters with his finger, close his eyes and try to visualise the word shape while saying it. Use only 4 or 5 words at a time. Don't labour the exercise too much or you will lose his interest.

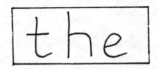

Point out the shapes of distinctive letters. An **s**, for example, looks (and sounds) like a snake and **I** is like a tall, thin man standing straight up.

The Alphabet

Some parents write out the alphabet on a long piece of card in both script letters and capitals. At bedtime they and the child sing all the letters after they have read a story together. Script should be kept separate from capitals.

Essential Words

Certain words should be learnt. They include: Stop, Danger, Police, the child's own name and address written out carefully, and the days of the week — Sunday, Monday, Tuesday, Wednesday, Thursday, Friday, Saturday. Many parents paste these words up on the bedroom wall and talk about them from time to time.

Key Words

These are words that occur most commonly in text. I have used them very effectively indeed in accelerating the progress of children who were failing to read at school. The first 12 words are extremely important. Some of them occur in reading books a thousand times more frequently than many nouns.

First Group:

a   and   he   I   in   is   it   of   that   the   to   was

The most effective way to teach these words is to write them large with a felt tip pen as separate words on card and teach them in the 'flash-card' manner. Teach only 4 or 5 at a time.

Second group:

all   as   at   be   but   are   for   had   have   him

his   not   on   one   said   so   they   we   with   you

Third group:

about   back   been   before   big   by   call   came

could   did   do   down   first   from   got   go   has

her   here   if   into   just   like   little   look   make

made   me   more   much   must   my   new   no

now   off   old   on   only   or   other   our   out

over   right   see   she   some   their   them   then

there   this   two   up   want   well   went   were

what   when   where   which   who   will   your

You will notice the absence of nouns in this list. Later, when writing, children need nouns for their stories. The graded vocabulary list gives the most commonly used nouns in writing as:

house   daddy   garden   girl   tree   car   boat   school

flower   train   man   night   boy   doll   shop   mother

dog   baby   snow

Phonics

A child will learn to read many words using the above methods. Quite soon, though, he will need to sound out letters for himself.

Simply going through the alphabet is useful but grouping sounds together is a more interesting way to teach them. It also ties in with spelling. The Phonic Alphabet is illustrated on the next page.

One system used by many schools is the teaching scheme called Letterland. Every letter is portrayed by a special 'picto-gram' character and each of these represents the sound of the letter. Thus there are characters such as Bouncy Ben, Dippy Duck and Fireman Fred all of whom help change abstract symbols into real-life letters.

Initial letters

These can be taught by choosing a consonant, C for example, and finding simple words that begin with it. Write the word on card and pair it, if possible, with a picture. Get your child to trace the letter with his finger, to close his eyes and visualise the letter associated with an object (for example C with 'cat' or 'car').

The C group could include Cup, Car, Cot, Cap, Cat. Write the initial letter large on the card: **Cup**.

Vowels

These can also be learnt by grouping words with similar letters. This is dealt with fully in the spelling section, as it is here that children often muddle sounds.

When your child has a good knowledge of individual letter sounds you can introduce 'blends'. Making up words from such combinations is a useful exercise. Use cl, cr, br, bl, dr, fl, gr, gl, pr, pl, st, sp, tr, sw, sh, ch.

Later, vowel combinations are introduced: ar, oo, or, er, oi, oy, ou, ow, ear.

Finally, endings of words are included: –ip, –ag, –ash, –op, –ill, –og, –ush, –ab, –im, –in, –an, –ink, –ot, –ick, –ect.

Reading along with your child

Reading along with your child is extremely important because it encourages his interest. If your child does not wish to attempt reading with you do not press the issue, but continue reading while you trace the words with your finger. Stop frequently to discuss what is happening in the story and to look and talk about the pictures. The interest in reading text will develop a

confirmed reader and lead to a child who is good at English. The mechanics will only teach her to read words with a superficial understanding while reading helps comprehension.

Books, books and more books

A house which has many books generally has a child who reads a lot. For my own children I scoured jumble sales, libraries and bookshops for interesting books. John was interested in Enid Blyton (from the age of 3 to 7 or 8) so over the years I built up a small library of her books and later Roald Dahl and a hundred other authors together with many non-fiction books on every subject under the sun. Consequently, all the children are exceptional at reading and writing stories. Where children are not interested in reading, I encourage parents to buy picture books or to use the local library.

Starter books These should have few words, be about real life or imaginative, have a story with significant events and humour or conflict. They should also have well-drawn and interesting pictures with story elements to discuss in them. The following is a list of books with outstanding appeal. (The hardback edition has been listed but most are also available in paperback editions.)

Adams, Ken, (illus. Val Biro), *When I was your Age*, Simon and Schuster 1991

Ahlberg, Allan, *Happy Families* series, Viking Kestrel/Puffin; *Red nose readers*, Walker Books

Ahlberg, Janet and Allan, *Each Peach Pear Plum*, Oliver and Boyd 1989; *Funny-bones*, Heinemann 1980

Briggs, Raymond, *The Snowman* storybooks, Hamish Hamilton

Browne, Anthony, *Gorilla*, Julia MacRae Books 1983

Bruna, Dick, *I am a Clown*, Methuen 1976 (and other Bruna titles)

Burningham, John, *Avocado Baby*, Cape 1982; *Little Books* series, Cape

Carle, Eric, *The Very Hungry Caterpillar*, Hamish Hamilton 1970

Collins' *Beginner Books for Beginning Readers* series; *I Can Read it all by Myself*, Beginner Books series

Hill, Eric, *Spot* series, Heinemann

Hutchins, Pat, *Don't Forget the Bacon*, The Bodley Head 1976
Keats, Ezra Jack, *Whistle for Willie*, The Bodley Head 1966
Ladybird Books *Key Words* Reading Scheme (especially the fairy
    tale books)
Lodge, Bernard, *The Grand Old Duke of York*, Magnet
McKee, David, *Not Now, Bernard*, Andersen Press 1980 (This is
my all-time favourite picture book.)
Minarik, Else Holmelund, *Little Bear*, World's Work 1965
(*I Can Read* series)
Potter, Beatrix, *The Tale of Peter Rabbit*, Frederick Warne 1987
Ross, Tony, *Naughty Nigel*, Andersen Press 1982
Sendak, Maurice, *Where the Wild Things Are*, The Bodley Head
    1967
Vipont, Elfrida, (illus. Raymond Briggs), *The Elephant and the
    Bad Baby*, Hamish Hamilton 1969
World's Work *I Can Read* books
Zion, Gene, and Graham, Margaret Bloy, *Harry the Dirty Dog*,
    The Bodley Head 1960

Rhymes and Fairy Stories
Boswell, Hilda, *A Treasury of Fairy Tales*, Collins; *A Treasury
    of Nursery Rhymes*, Collins
Corrin, Sara and Stephen, Ed., *The Faber Book of Favourite
    Fairy Tales*, Faber 1988
Ladybird Book of Rhymes, Ladybird Books
Mother Goose Collection of Nursery Rhymes, Oxford
    University Press

Poetry Some poems go down very well. Try 'Matilda Who Told
Lies, and was Burned to Death' by Hilaire Belloc and 'Adventures of Isabel' by Ogden Nash, both from *A Catalogue of
Comic Verse*, edited by Rolf Harris (Hodder 1988). The following is a list of some other books your child might enjoy:

Britton, James, *An Anthology of Verse for Children*, Vols 1–4,
    Oxford University Press
Harrison, Michael and Clark, Christopher Stuart, Ed., *The
Oxford Book of Christmas Poems*, Oxford University Press,
1983; *The Oxford Treasury of Children's Poems*, Oxford
University Press 1988
Ireson, Barbara, Ed., *The Faber Book of Nursery Verse* 1983

McGough, Roger, and Rosen, Michael, *You Tell Me*, Viking 1989
McGough, Roger, Ed., *The Kingfisher Book of Comic Verse*, Kingfisher 1986
Milligan, Spike, *Startling Verse for All the Family*, Penguin 1989
Nash, Ogden, *Custard and Company*, Blake, Quentin, Ed., Penguin 1981
Nicoll, Helen, Ed., *Poems for 7 Year Olds and Under*, Viking Kestrel 1985
Opie, Iona and Peter, Ed., *The Oxford Book of Children's Verse*, Oxford University Press, 1973
Prelutsky, Jack, *The Walker Book of Poetry for Children*, Walker Books 1983
Rosen, Michael, *Mind Your Own Business*, André Deutsch 1974

Picture/Word Cards
A.B.C. Wallchart, Ladybird Books 1987
Baby's First Board Book (Blue Book and Pink Book) World International Publishing 1990
Ladybird learning frieze
Spot's First Picture Word Cards Michael Stanfield

Videos
Spot's Alphabet (A-B-C), Tempo Video
Learn with Sooty series, Thames Television International

Early Readers These books are for children who are reading reasonably well and need consolidation.

Biro, Val, *Gumdrop* books, Hodder
Blyton, Enid, *The Magic Faraway Tree*, Beaver Books 1985; *The Adventures of the Wishing Chair*, 1937; *Mr. Meddle's Muddles*, Dean 1970; the new *Noddy* series, Macdonald 1990; and there are many other books to choose from.
Brisley, Joyce Lankester, *Milly Molly Mandy* series, Harrap
Dahl, Roald, and Blake, Quentin, *The Enormous Crocodile*, Cape 1978
Dahl, Roald, *Fantastic Mr. Fox*, Allen and Unwin 1970; *James and the Giant Peach*, Unwin Hyman 1990; *The Magic Finger*, Unwin Hyman 1989

Edwards, Dorothy, *My Naughty Little Sister*, Methuen 1969;
More Naughty Little Sister Stories, Methuen 1971

Milne, A.A., *The World of Pooh*, Methuen 1926

Murphy, Jill, *A Bad Spell for the Worst Witch*, Viking Kestrel
1984; *The Worst Witch Strikes Again*, Viking Kestrel 1988

Storr, C., *Clever Polly and the Stupid Wolf*, Penguin 1967

Tomlinson, Jill, *The Owl who was Afraid of the Dark*, Methuen
1968

Townson, H., *The Great Ice-Cream Crime*, Andersen Press
1981

ENGLISH: EARLY WRITING

You can teach your child to trace over the letters of the alphabet
using a crayon – make them big because, at first, his writing will
be big. If he has difficulty get him to practise the patterns below.
Most letter shapes are covered by these forms.

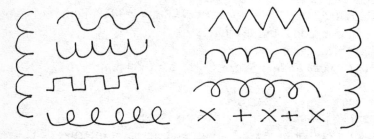

In order to endorse a multisensory approach, get him to trace
letters in a sand-tray or to form them in playdoh. Big lower-case
letters cut out in card can help him to appreciate letter form.
Ensure you show him how the letters are written and that he
forms them in the correct direction.

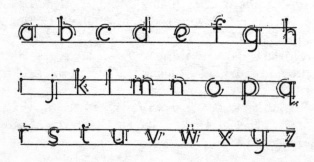

Finally, you might like to draw the letters in the form of dots which he can then join up:

Start with the letter c, first, or o. Children seem to find these the easiest to write. Emphasise and enlarge the letters to explain the difference between b and d, and n and h because small children find this hard to spot. Philip, a capable third-year junior, still occasionally makes mistakes with these letters.

Later, you will be able to introduce the copying of words and even sentences into your child's reading programme. Eventually, he should be able to write a few words, or a sentence, beneath a picture he has drawn.

Other Writing

To complete the output part of language for this age it will be necessary to encourage creative writing, diary writing and other written comments on real life.

As soon as your child is able, encourage him to keep a diary or scrapbook. Even if he writes in it only once a week it is useful. He can write below pictures he cuts out, write about trips to castles, cathedrals, and on holidays. He can write a short sentence or two to Santa Claus, to auntie or grandma. Do not worry too much about spelling at this stage, or even full stops. This will be taught separately and will improve as he writes more.

Deer arntie,
                Fank yu for
the present it wos ooseless
but yu ar stil kind
to send it
                Luv Benny

When he has watched a particularly interesting film or programme on television, or seen a Walt Disney cartoon on video, read an interesting picture book, or enjoyed a story on tape, get your child to write a few words about it. Ask him to try to picture each scene before he writes anything down. Visualising scenes in one's mind makes the writing come alive. Sandra, who is 7, had never written anything of any note until she saw a video of Walt Disney's *Cinderella*. For the first time in her life the writing really flowed as I saw her translate the images in her mind into living words.

Writing about Investigations

The science experiments children do at home also provide useful material to write about. This could include watching cress seedlings grow, writing down temperatures, and making a list of insects and plants in the garden. (*See* page 60.)

Handwriting

Some parents are very concerned about handwriting at too early an age. It should be developed over a matter of years and rigorous training in letterwriting at 5 should be avoided. However, some children enjoy copying words from books.

There are several points your child should be made aware of, for instance, that **p**, **q**, and **g** all sit on the line, and, of course, letters and numbers written back to front should be corrected as already mentioned. (Many parents are horrified when their child writes back to front. It does not mean that your child is backward.) Initially words are written on blank pages because children like to write big and express themselves freely; only when a child is competent at writing is lined paper introduced.

Capitals and Full Stops

The idea of a sentence as an entity is best taught at first through exercises. However, it does no harm to point out to an older infant child where to put capitals. Capitals occur in place names and other proper nouns as well as at the beginning of sentences while full stops occur at the end of sentences.

Word Meanings

These can be taught through real-life objects, real-life experiences, discussion, through simple crosswords, fitting words into sentences, opposites, rearranging words to make a meaningful sentence and unjumbling the letters of mixed-up words.

Spelling Lists by Groups

Only early phonic words and 'blends' that introduce words are given for the 5–7 age group. Spelling should not be introduced until a child can read. A very effective way to teach spelling is to ask a child to cover the word after looking carefully at it and asking him to visualise it. Then get him to say the word several times tracing the word out with his finger or writing it down, if necessary several times.

Short vowel words

Group 1

at	man	bat	bad	bag	cam	bap
an	can	cat	cad	fag	jam	cap
	ban	fat	dad	gag	ham	gap
	fan	hat	fad	lag	ram	lap
	pan	mat	had	rag	sam	map
	ran	pat	lad	tag		nap
	tan	rat	mad	wag		rap
		sat	sad	nag		tap

Group 2

off	not	pod	bog	cop
on	cot	cod	hog	mop
of	hot		dog	lop
	pot		log	top
	dot			hop
	rot			
	tot			

Group 3

men	bet	bed	beg	hem
den	met	led	leg	
pen	pet			
ten	set			
	vet			
	let			
	jet			

Group 4

in	bin	bit	bid	big	him	hip
it	din	fit	did	dig	rim	pip
	tin	hit	hid	fig	dim	lip
	fin	kit	kid	pig		sip
	gin	lit	lid	wig		tip
	pin	pit		gig		rip
	sin	sit				nip
	tin					
	win					

Group 5

up	bun	but	bud	bug	gum	cup
	fun	cut	dud	dug	hum	pup
	gun	gut	mud	rug	mum	sup
	nun	hut		hug	rum	
	pun	nut		mug	tum	
	run	rut		tug	sum	
	sun					

(**Note to parents**: emphasise the difference between 'of' and 'off' in Group 2 by putting them in short sentences.)

At this stage it is very useful for your child to learn to spell the first key words as well as being able to read them, especially *the, to, and, I, was, there, here.*

The spelling of the number words can be linked to practical maths activities as can the names of shapes. The spellings of words used in mathematical activities described later should also be written down and learnt.

Double 'blends' of letters

*bri*dge	*gra*ss	*tr*ee
*bl*ow	*gl*ove	*tw*in
*cr*own	*pr*am	*sh*op
*cl*own	*pl*ate	*ch*op or *ch*in
*dr*op	*sl*ip	moon
*fr*og	*sp*ot	*fee*t
*fl*u	*sw*ing	*qu*een

Magic 'e' This can be explained at age 7. It turns *rid* to *ride*, *rod* to *rode*, *hug* to *huge*, *hop* to *hope*.

Reference
- Television programmes like *Sesame Street* and *Words and Pictures*
- Schonell spelling books (*see* page 93)
- 'Little Professor' spelling game, Texas instruments

For older infants who are very good at reading, 'Junior Scrabble' might be appropriate, although it is usually only older juniors who can cope with difficult words.

Educational Videos (available from W.H. Smith and other High Street shops.)
- *Helping your child to read*
- *My Sesame Street Home Video: Learning about numbers; Learning about letters and getting ready to read*

EARLY MATHEMATICS

Sorting
This is an activity that should precede counting. A good set of children's wooden bricks is useful well before your child goes to school because then he can sort for size, shape and colour. The use of three-dimensional objects is also a very memorable experience. A child will learn much about the properties of shapes simply by handling them, and that knowledge will be invaluable as he moves through school Maths.

Sort for size   *Sort for shape*

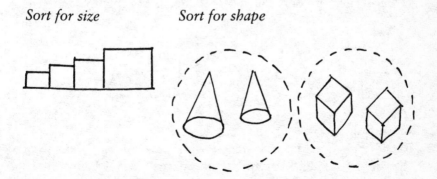

Sort for colour

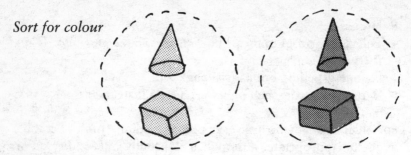

Associated words Many word meanings can be taught using a simple set of bricks. Here are some words that can be used when doing the sorting activites:

circle   square   rectangle   cube   cuboid   prism

triangle   pentagon   hexagon   cone   pyramid   left

right   middle   next   big   bigger   biggest   tall

taller   tallest   wide   wider   widest   short   shorter

shortest   small   smaller   smallest

long   longer   longest   round   straight   curve

right-angle   pointed   edge   corner   face   red   orange

yellow   green   blue   purple   violet   black   white

grey   brown

Pairing Games like 'Snap', 'Whist', and 'Happy Families' illustrate this principle. By 5 a child should easily be able to pair knives with forks and cups with saucers.

Ordering This gives the idea of a sequence or repetitive pattern:

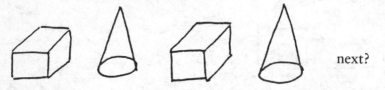

next?

Counting

This is best done in easy stages, with real objects. Count to 5, then to 10, 15, and so on. Use an abacus (with 10 rows of 10 beads in each row), buttons, marbles, children's bricks of similar size and shape, or coins of the same denomination.

Some children get stuck on certain numbers, usually those between 12 and 19.

When your child is counting easily you can introduce written numbers, always making sure that he equates the written number with a number of similar objects or pictures.

1 ·   2 · ·   3 · · ·   4 · · · ·

5 · · · · ·   6 · · · · · ·   7 · · · · · · ·

8 · · · · · · · ·   9 · · · · · · · · ·

10 · · · · · · · · ·

Until your child knows all his numbers, for future activities on paper always write the numbers down for him to refer to. Do not be dismayed if he writes his numbers back to front – this often happens with 2, 3, 5 and 9 and may continue for quite some time.

Some children really take to counting. John, at 2½ years, vowed to count to 1000 before he fell asleep at night. I could hear him in his bed, 'one hundred and twenty-six, one hundred and twenty-seven . . .' He never made it past 200.

You should take counting as far as you can without pressurising. For a child to know about 'big' numbers is important. As I said above a good abacus (a calculating frame with movable beads on wires) is invaluable for this.

Aids
- 'Dominoes' is a useful game to teach matching numbers. Make sure that the dots on the blocks are big and clear.
- 'Spot's First Pairs Game' (Michael Stanfield) from all good toyshops.
- Learning Bricks (available from The Home Education Centre Limited, 130 Manchester Road, Swinton, Manchester M27).
- Dot-to-dot books teach the written numbers but be sure that the number range is not beyond your child.

- Draughts and Chess will give a certain spatial awareness, a sense of angle, and will train your child in visualising (since he will have to think several moves ahead).

Adding Sums

For some time numbers should carry a picture appendage, or be associated with real objects like buttons or coins. Simon is 6, already 'failing' at school, and is needing much practice with counting using real-life objects. He gets confused if objects are not set out in a straight line.

Initially, when teaching addition, do sums *without* symbols.

Using fingers Fingers are one of the best aids for counting and for learning early addition and subtraction. When adding, show your child how to hold up a finger for each number. You should also put the picture appendage (e.g. stickmen or dots) with each number:

Other ways of beginning addition are to put wooden bricks one on top of the other, to use buttons or counters and to make cards with pictures on and then push them together:

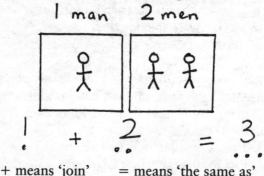

+ means 'join'   = means 'the same as'

The abacus is also a most useful aid in addition.

The Number Line Many text books use the number line which should be written *vertically* on the page and not horizontally as many schools practise. By writing the line vertically the child begins to understand that 'bigger' is *up* the line to 10 and 'smaller' is *down* to 0, and lower negative numbers in due course. If a child is, for example, trying to add 2 plus 3 tell him to 'Start at 2 (point to 2), count on 3' until he reaches 5. Emphasise that you do not start the counting on the 2. Also explain the presence of *zero*.

More, more than This is a different concept to straightforward addition. Children certainly have difficulty linking the two. Using two sets of wooden blocks or buttons explain that:

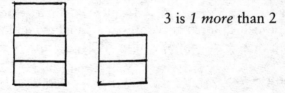

3 is *1 more* than 2

Number bonds to 10 Ask your child to find out how many sums he can make with 3, 4, 5, 6, 7, 8, 9, 10 blocks. For example, bonds to 5 should be:

$$0 + 5 = 5 \quad 1 + 4 = 5 \quad 2 + 3 = 5 \quad 3 + 2 = 5$$
$$4 + 1 = 5 \quad 5 + 0 = 5$$

This may lead to the discovery that:

$$2 + 3 = 3 + 2 \qquad 1 + 4 = 4 + 1$$

These patterns are extremely useful in real life.

Variations

Explain that there are different ways of writing sums, both horizontal and vertical.

$$2 + 3 = 5$$

$$2 \xrightarrow{+3} 5$$

$$2 + 3 = \boxed{5}$$

Number jigsaws These can extend addition activities and certainly make Maths more enjoyable. Fitting two pieces together completes the sum.

Dice games

- Throw two dice and see who can score the highest.
- 'Ludo' and 'Snakes and Ladders' help to extend counting (although children get confused in 'Snakes and Ladders' when they change direction) and furthers addition practice.

Taking Away

Similar activities to adding up should be used – using children's bricks, buttons, sweets, marbles, fingers, etc. before introducing symbols. Teach 'taking away' as just that – a removal of objects. Only introduce symbols when your child is used to the idea.

O   O   O   take away

$$3 - 1 = 2$$

As with addition you will need to introduce the number line and the idea of *less than* which as I have said causes difficulty with children who cannot visualise the missing object:

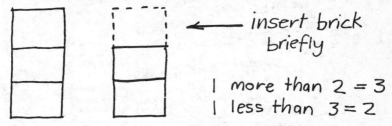

← ─── insert brick
briefly

1 more than 2 = 3
1 less than 3 = 2

Number rhymes and jingles These include songs such as '1, 2, 3, 4, 5 once I caught a fish alive . . .' and 'Ten green bottles . . .' and they certainly make counting more fun.

Placeholder This is quite simply a box for a number. The concept is almost an introduction to algebra. Some children are very good with:

$$\Box + 3 = 5$$
? ・・。 ・・・・・

The Two Times Table
This can be introduced practically with dolls, teddy bears (two legs on each) or buttons, and wooden bricks:

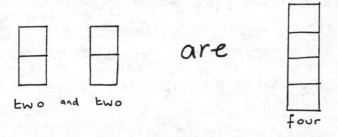

two and two   are   four

Later this can be expressed with symbols and pictures:

$$2 + 2 + 2 = 6$$
・・ ・・ 。・ ・。・・・・

Finally, a whole series can be introduced:

one   two   is   two
1 × 2 = ⊙   2

2 × 2 = ⊙ ⊙   4

3 × 2 = ⊙ ⊙ ⊙   6

4 × 2 = ⊙ ⊙ ⊙ ⊙   8

5 × 2 = ⊙ ⊙ ⊙ ⊙ ⊙   10

This format is extremely effective as it helps the child to really understand how the tables work. Later you can extend it to the Five and Ten Times tables. (*See* pages 99–100.)

1 × 2 = ⊙ 2

2 × 2 = ⊙ ⊙ 4

3 × 2 = ⊙ ⊙ ⊙ 6

4 × 2 = ⊙ ⊙ ⊙ ⊙ 8

5 × 2 = ⊙ ⊙ ⊙ ⊙ ⊙ 10

6 × 2 = ⊙ ⊙ ⊙ ⊙ ⊙ ⊙ 12

7 × 2 = ⊙ ⊙ ⊙ ⊙ ⊙ ⊙ ⊙ 14

8 × 2 = ⊙ ⊙ ⊙ ⊙ ⊙ ⊙ ⊙ ⊙ 16

9 × 2 = ⊙ ⊙ ⊙ ⊙ ⊙ ⊙ ⊙ ⊙ ⊙ 18

10 × 2 = ⊙ ⊙ ⊙ ⊙ ⊙ ⊙ ⊙ ⊙ ⊙ ⊙ 20

The number line also helps a child to count in twos:

Sharing

The concept of sharing can be explained by sharing sweets between yourself and your child. It is best, initially, to develop the sharing idea between *two* people. Only when he is clear about the concept should you move on to sharing among three.

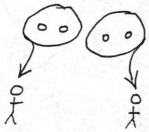

four sweets shared between two is two each

Later, symbols can be introduced:

$$4 \div 2 = 2$$

four shared by two = two

and

$$2 \overline{)4}^{\,2}$$

As a process children readily learn division as 'how many twos in four?'

◉ ◉   2 twos make 4

With larger numbers the idea of, say, 14 shared by two is difficult to visualise. Children prefer to change to 'how many twos in 14?' thus relating division to multiplication:

$$2 \overline{)14}^{\,7}$$

◉ ◉ ◉ ◉ ◉ ◉ ◉ = 7 twos make 14

The above also establishes another pattern of *reversing* operations:

$$7 \xleftrightarrow[\div 2]{\times 2} 14$$

Similarly they should know that:

$$2 \underset{-3}{\overset{+3}{\rightleftarrows}} 5$$

These are called *inverse* operations.

Shapes

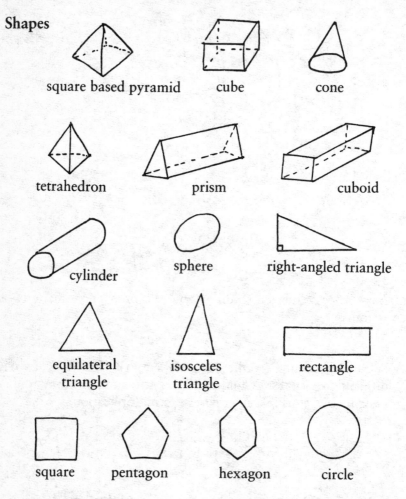

square based pyramid   cube   cone

tetrahedron   prism   cuboid

cylinder   sphere   right-angled triangle

equilateral
triangle   isosceles
triangle   rectangle

square   pentagon   hexagon   circle

Children of 7 should know most of the names of the above shapes.

Telling the time

Help your child to understand 'time' by relating the time on a clock face to his everyday life. But take this stage slowly and concentrate on making him aware of the passing of time. Talk about days and weeks and where you are in time. Relate months and seasons to birthdays or holidays and special events. Make a record or calendar.

Months of the year

January   February   March   April   May   June   July

August   September   October   November   December

'Thirty days have September, April, June and November. All the rest have 31 excepting February alone which has 28 days clear, and 29 in each leap year.'

Months on the Knuckles Tuck in the thumbs on each hand and say the months on and between each knuckle. Every 'knuckle month' has 31 days.

The Clock You will need a clock with movable hands and the numbers 1 to 12 written clearly on it.

(1) Make sure that your child is aware that one hand is *long* and the other *short*.
(2) Show him the hours: 'This is one o'clock.'
(3) Test him on some random o'clock times.
(4) Continue for some days or weeks until he is sure of these, then continue the same procedure with half-past, quarter-past, quarter-to. When testing, always include o'clock times as well as other times in saturation learning fashion.
(5) Teach your child that there are 60 minutes to the hour, 30 minutes to the half-hour, 15 minutes to the quarter, and 45 minutes to the three-quarter. This phase make take some time (maybe weeks, or months).
(6) Teach minutes *past* and *to* the hour. Children find counting back more difficult. Also, show your child how to count in *fives* round the clock.

One child of 6 (who is supposed to be remedial), recently introduced me to a novel way of doing addition and subtraction sums by using a clock.

For 9 + 8 = 17 he counted to 9, then started at 12 and counted *on* to 8 (10, 11 . . . 17), using the clock as a number line.

Fractions

Your child should get used to the idea of one-half, one-quarter and one-third by cutting cakes and showing pictures:

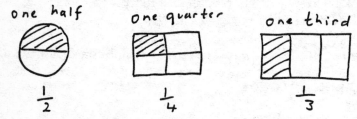

Some schools do not seem to emphasise strongly enough the division of 'one whole'. A child should have much more practice using real objects or using pictures. Also, at this stage it is important to point out something that confuses 11-year-olds:

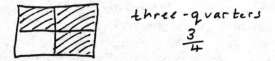

They do not have clearly in their minds the idea that:

$$\frac{1}{4} + \frac{1}{4} + \frac{1}{4} = \frac{3}{4}$$

Lack of practice with material is the reason. Children should also appreciate that half of 6 is 3.

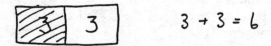

This should provide a link with 3 + 3 = 6.

   In work with much older children I am continually having to refer back pictorially to the divisions of one whole.

Investigations and graphs

Get your child to count how many chairs, tables and beds there are in the house. You can set his answers down for him in graphical form:

chairs h h h h h h h h

tables ⊓⊓ ⊓⊓ ⊓⊓ ⊓⊓ ⊓⊓ ⊓⊓

beds h⊓ h⊓ h⊓ h⊓

Ask questions like 'How many more chairs than beds are there?' There are many variations on this theme.

Money

Use real money to teach this, although plastic money, bought from a toy shop, is a good alternative. Eventually, your child will have to learn that:

$$2p = 1p + 1p$$

$$5p = 1p + 1p + 1p + 1p + 1p$$

$$5p = 2p + 2p + 1p$$

$$5p = 2p + 1p + 1p + 1p$$

To overcome the difficulty that he will have in visualising 2p as 1p + 1p, when counting, get him to tap twice on the 2p:

1p	+	1p	+	2p	=	4p
one tap		one tap		two taps		four taps

After your child can count using 1p coins, move on to include 2p coins, 5p coins, and 10p coins. Practice is the answer to knowing many operations and real-life practice must include shopping.

Shopping Your child will need a play till, objects marked with prices (mark these low at first – 2p, 5p, 3p), and money. Shopping needs to be taught in stages:

(a) Get him only to give over the money for one particular toy.
(b) Get him to add up the cost of two objects. You are the shop keeper for these activities.
(c) He gives you say, 5p for a 2p object. You show him how you work out the change, even writing down the sum. You are still the shopkeeper.
(d) This is the big day: he is the shopkeeper! He has to add up the cost of items, and later, he has to work out the change. Show him how to write the sums down:

$$\text{book} \quad + \quad \text{teddy}$$
$$3p \quad + \quad 4p \quad = \quad 7p$$

Change (from, say, 10p):
$$10p \quad - \quad 7p \quad = \quad 3p$$

The whole process has to be taken at a steady pace but by 7 it is possible for him to act as shopkeeper competently. Clear presentation and explanation is important because shopping is essentially a problem-solving exercise.

Tens and Units

When your child is counting well to 100, you will need to introduce tens and units. Eleven buttons can be laid out:

Tens (t)   Units (u)

With the abacus, real-life objects, and later pictures, you can show:

two tens	no units	three tens	no units
Tens (t)	units (u)	Tens (t)	units (u)
2	0	3	0

Measurement

Stage 1 Teach your child to measure distances, weights and volumes *without* using units. For distance measure with feet, handspans and steps. Encourage your child to weigh things on a balance. He can then see when one thing is heavier than another, and even read off the number on the scale. To balance both sides must be equal.

He can investigate to see how many cups will fill Mummy's plastic jug. If it is graduated, he can read off the number.

Stage 2 When your child has grasped the concepts of length, weight and volume introduce him to units.

Length He can measure using a ruler with centimetres clearly marked off – books, tables, etc. – to the *nearest* whole centimetre. Make a metre rule with stiff card, marking off the centimetres. He can measure distances (the front room) and heights (the table top) in metres and centimetres. He can *estimate* and confirm his guess on lengths. 'Rounding-up' gives a good notion of remainders. Tell him we can write 1 centimetre as 1 cm and 1 metre as 1 m.

Angles

The understanding or sense of angle can be conveyed to a child by the opening of a door. The further the door opens, the bigger is the angle. Placing two rulers together at the ends also demonstrates the concept:

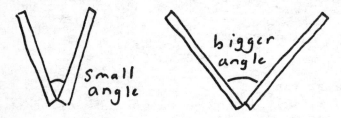

Similarly, garden shears, scissors and other household objects can be used (by you!) to show this.

Compass points Another way of conveying sense of *angle*, and one that also teaches the idea of *rotation*, is teaching the points

of the compass. You can either mark these in chalk on the garden path, or on a large sheet of stiff paper and lay it on the floor. Your child can then stand on the centre point and turn to face in various directions.

Explain that turning from North to East (N to E) is a turn through a right angle, from North to South (N to S), through two right angles. John at 3½ years old found this great fun. He found the concept useful in Maths right up to A level.

Reflection

Take a large rectangular sheet of paper and fold it down the middle. Ask your child to paint on one side of the parting, then fold it to produce an image.

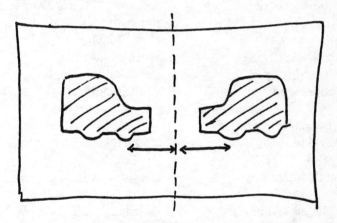

Point out that the distance to the centre line is the same from equivalent points of object and image. Sam brought me literally tens of pictures done in this way. 'Look what I've done!' he claimed, proudly, while his mother stood on one side wringing her hands, and wondering where the next piece of paper was coming from.

Another useful exercise is to get your child to divide capital letters with a line so that symmetry can be explored:

MUSIC

At 5–6 years of age children should revive their knowledge of nursery songs and jingles. Songs with a range of less than an octave are best.

Selection of songs
Nursery Rhymes

Baa, baa, black sheep
Bobby Shafto
Ding-dong bell
Here we go round the
   Mulberry Bush
Hey diddle diddle
Hickory, Dickory Dock
Hot Cross buns
Incey Wincey Spider
Jack and Jill
Lavender's blue

London Bridge
One, two, three, four, five
O dear, what can the matter be?
Oranges and lemons
Pop! goes the weasel
Ring-a-ring o'roses
See-Saw, Margery Daw
Sing a song of sixpence
This Old Man
Three Blind Mice
Twinkle, twinkle, little star
Yankee Doodle

Traditional and Modern

A-Roving
Billy Boy
Blow the man down
Clementine
Cockles and Mussels
Danny Boy
Dashing away
Donkey Riding
Early one morning
The Eton Boating Song
The Old Grey Goose (Go tell
   Aunt Rhody)
Green grow the rushes, O!
I'd like to teach the world to
   sing
If you're happy

Li'l Liza Jane
The Poacher
The Little Brown Jug
Looby Loo
Merrily we roll
Michael Finnigan
Muffin
My Bonnie lies over the Ocean
Oh, soldier, soldier
Scarborough Fair
Sing a rainbow
Skye Boat song
Strawberry Fair
Sur le pont
There were ten in a bed
Yellow Submarine

Christmas songs and carols

Away in a Manger

I saw three ships

Jingle bells

Rudolph the Red Nosed
  Reindeer

Silent Night

We wish you a Merry
  Christmas

Records and cassettes
Children's Choice – CRS Records
Hello Children Everywhere – Original Artists

Film songs and videos   Disney films include:
Alice in Wonderland, Bambi, Cinderella, Dumbo, Fantasia, Lady and the Tramp, 101 Dalmatians, Pinocchio, The Sleeping Beauty, Snow White and the seven dwarfs.
These, and the songs, are a wonderful stimulation for writing and drawing pictures.
  Other cartoon films of note are:

Gulliver's Travels, The Lion, The Witch and the Wardrobe, The Wizard of Oz.

Music Books
Hart, Jane, Ed., *Sing a Song of Sixpence: The Best Song Book Ever*, Gollancz 1983
Harrop, Beatrice, Ed., *Apusskidu: Songs for Children*, A. & C. Black 1975; *Sing Hey Diddle Diddle: 66 Nursery Rhymes with Traditional Tunes*, A. & C. Black 1983
Strawberry Fair: 51 Traditional Songs, A. & C. Black 1985

Learning an Instrument Most children start with a recorder. The violin is difficult to learn. If your child shows talent you may wish to send him to a tutor who can enter him for exams in due course.

Music Examination Boards
• Associated Board, London
• London College of Music
• Trinity College, London

Exam pieces can be obtained from music shops.

Books for Learning

Piano:
Michael Aaron, Piano Course series, Belwin-Mills/International Music Publications

Baker, Kenneth, *The Complete Piano Player* books, Music Sales
John W. Schawn Piano Course series, International Music Publications
Waterman, Fanny, *Piano Lessons* series, Faber 1967

Recorder:
Bush, Roger, *Abracadabra Recorder: Graded Songs and Tunes*, Books 1–4, A. & C. Black 1982
Pitts, John, *Recorder from the Beginning*, Books 1–3, Arnold Wheaton 1981–4
Priestley, Edmund, *School Recorder Books* Book 1, Arnold Wheaton 1962

Clarinet:
Harvey, Paul, *The Complete Clarinet Player*, Music Sales
Hesforth, Paul, *Tune a Day for Clarinet*, International Music Publications
Wastall, Peter, *Learn as you Play Clarinet*, Boosey & Hawkes 1979
Appelbaum, Samuel, *Stringbuilder*, Belwin-Mills/International Music Publications
Eta Cohen Violin Method Books 1–3, Novello
Davey, Peter, *Abracadabra Violin: The Way to Learn Through Songs and Times*, A. & C. Black 1986

<u>ART</u>

If your child shows a great inclination towards this subject you will need to provide materials to work with.

Pencils and crayons
- *Pencils* From 8B (smudgy) to 8H (very hard). For drawing 2B–4B are best, while H or 2H are better for guide-lines.
- *Charcoal* Good for drawing but smudgy.
- *Wax crayons* Short, thick crayons for general work and narrow, blunt crayons for colouring.
- *Pastels* These are expensive but produce a richness in colour. Pastels and *chalks* smudge and must be fixed by a spray for permanence.
- *Coloured pencils* These include some which, when dipped in water, produce a watercolour effect.
- *Rubbers/Erasers* Plastic is more effective than rubber.

Paper
- *Cartridge paper* All-purpose.
- *Sugar paper* Useful for painting and cheap.

Paints The main colours for use in artwork are black, white (for mixing), yellow, red, blue and purple.
- *Powder paints* are the cheapest. There are packs for small children (e.g. Berol). *Ready mixed* powder paint is also available in plastic containers e.g. W.H. Smith, Galt.
- *Block* This is more expensive and colours get carried from colour to colour more easily.
- *Acrylic (plastic) colours* These adhere to any surface without priming (unlike oils). Use methylated spirits to remove paint from brushes.

Brushes Thick, long hog-hair is best for general work.

Adhesives Pastes are cheap (e.g. Polycell). Copydex is good for mounting. Polymer glue sticks just about anything (including clothes!). Non-toxic adhesives are safer and children should be supervised when using other pastes. Glue sticks are also useful for paper and card. They are clean and quick (e.g. PrittStick).

Materials for 3-D work
- *Papier Mâché* This is made by dipping strips of newspaper into paste and forming a shape. It takes several days to dry.
- *Plasticine*, reusable dough such as playstuff or *playdoh* and *clay* can also be used for modelling.
- *Polyfilla* This can be painted on when the object being modelled or the papier mâché is dry.

Reference
Foster, P. *Drawing*, Usborne 1981; *Painting*, Usborne 1981
Pluckrose, A. *Crayons*, Franklin Watts 1987; *Paints*, Franklin Watts 1989

HISTORY AND GEOGRAPHY

This is best done in the local area through visits to the library, local museum and churches. During holidays and trips out, you should visit castles, historic houses, cathedrals and museums with your child. When travelling you can show him on the map where you are going. When you return from visits encourage him to write about them in his diary.

SCIENCE

Most ideas in science are concerned with the appreciation of a principle and word meanings.

Growth of a seedling Your child can investigate the growth of cress seeds or peas. Sow the seeds in damp sawdust or soil in a container on a window sill. Let your child watch and talk about what happens daily, taking out odd seedlings to look at and, with an older child, measure them. He can record what happens in a diary. Explain root, stem and leaves.

Variety of Life

In the garden In the summer encourage your child to collect all the small creatures he can find (ants, beetles, earthworms, spiders, harvestmen, caterpillars, woodlice, ladybirds etc.). Talk to your child about each animal, mentioning words such as *insect* (which has six legs) and *worm* (which is divided into segments). Point out both similarities and differences. Equip yourself with a good reference book and explain how a caterpillar transforms itself into a beautiful butterfly – your child may be able to find a caterpillar in the chrysalis stage. Read *The Very Hungry Caterpillar* by Eric Carle (Hamish Hamilton 1970) with him. Tell him how bugs provide food for other animals and also help keep the soil healthy. You should also make him aware that some insects, such as bees, wasps, centipedes, some beetles and spiders, can bite or sting and should not be touched.

Fruit and vegetables Your child can look at the fruit and vegetables you have in your larder. Explain to him how fruits contain seeds that can grow into new plants. Try examining the following: an orange, banana, blackberry, blackcurrant, cherry, tomato, pea, nuts, apple, pear, mushroom, potato, cabbage, onion, carrot.

In the park or in the countryside Let your child discover the wide variety of trees, bushes and plants. Tell him how at certain times of the year trees discharge seeds which have grown 'wings' and are blown by the wind or how the seeds in the fruits may be carried away by birds or animals. If you can find some pine trees children love examining and collecting fir cones. And, of course, collecting conkers from the horse-chestnut tree in the autumn provides much fun. Let your child collect a variety of things, such as leaves of different shapes and different types of grasses, to bring home and then draw and write about them.

You should also make your child aware that some things are poisonous. For example, many berries, bulbs, toadstools (a few are deadly) and some leaves. The following is a list of the most common poisonous trees and plants:

Apple tree	Holly	Narcissus
Autumn Crocus	Horse-chestnut tree	Oak tree
Belladonna Lily	Hyacinth	Oleander
Bleeding Heart	Hydrangea	Privet
Cherry tree	Iris	Rhododendron
Christmas Rose	Ivy	Rhubarb
Daffodil	Laburnum	Snowdrop
Daphne	Larkspur	Sweet pea
Foxglove	Laurel	Tomato leaves
Fly Agaric	Lily of the Valley	Wisteria
Mushroom	Morning Glory	Yew

Birds in the garden Encourage your child to observe the various birds that come to a bird table. A good reference book is invaluable. Here are a few suggestions:

Andrews, John, *Birds of Home and Garden*, Brian Todd Publishing House 1989

Gooders, John, *Field Guide to the Birds of Britain & Ireland*, Kingfisher Books 1989

Greenoak, Francesca, *Birds in Towns*, A. & C. Black 1979

At the Zoo There is a great deal to talk to your child about the Zoo. Point out the wide variety of animals. Older infants can be made aware of animals without backbones (such as insects, worms, crabs) and those with backbones (for example, fish, amphibians, reptiles, birds and mammals).

At the seaside The sea is full of life. A walk along the beach and pottering in rock pools can reveal seaweed, fishes, jelly-fish, crabs, ragworm and many other creatures.

Reference
Attenborough, David, *Discovering Life on Earth*, Collins 1981
Walters, Martin, *A Pocket Book of Animals*, Grisewood and
    Dempsey 1981
Usborne *First Nature* Books
Usborne *Mysteries and Marvels* series
The Usborne Nature-trail Omnibus, 1978
Usborne *Spotter's Guides* (e.g. *The Seashore*)

Television programmes such as 'Trials of Life', 'The Really Wild
    Show', 'Animal Magic', 'Country File', 'Fragile Earth',
    'Survival'

Parts of the body Your child should know all these: head, arm, leg, hand, foot, finger, toe, neck, eye, ear, mouth, nose, chest, stomach, bottom, knee, elbow, chin, lips, nails, skin, hair.

Health and hygiene At this age, your child must be aware of various aspects of health, such as:
- *Good food* It gives you energy, keeps you healthy and lets you grow.
- *Exercise* It strengthens the muscles and exercises the heart and lungs.
- *Teeth* Brushing his teeth to get rid of food particles after a meal will prevent germs growing there. Explain that dirty teeth decay. Sweet foods should be avoided.
- *Good health* Point out some aspects of good health. Explain that immunization prevents disease and is carried out by vaccination, or inoculation normally through an injection. Washing cuts helps to remove dirt which causes infection. Flies spread disease by carrying 'germs' from dung onto food and contaminating it. Food can decay and become

contaminated with bacteria which causes food poisoning. Hands should always be washed after going to the bathroom.
- *Rest* Sleep helps to keep the mind and body healthy.

People are different Point out the differences in people: eye colour, hair colour, shape, height, feet/hand size, skin colour, child/adult differences.

Waste products This is connected with pollution. Explain that the build up of waste products is a big problem – from car exhausts, the toilet, dustbins, people burning rubbish to factories dumping their waste in rivers.

Squashing, stretching and bending Show how squashing and stretching can affect a lump of plasticine. Compare how much easier it is to bend a wooden ruler than a stone or brick. Point out that other materials such as string, metal, sand, water, oil have different properties.

Sorting materials Get your child to sort materials according to various criteria: hardness, heaviness etc.

Heating and cooling Your child will be interested when you explain how heating a kettle of water makes the 'drops' of water move about faster and faster as the water boils and then escape as *steam*. Point out that if water is made very cold it turns into ice, snow or frost.

The seasons and the weather Knowledge of the seasons is important. Mention some of the things that happen in each season.
- *Winter* This is a time when the weather is cold. Christmas is in December. Some animals (e.g. bears) go to sleep and hibernate during the winter months.
- *Spring* Plants start to grow. The blossom on trees flowers.
- *Summer* The weather is hotter. Fruits develop and more flowers blossom.
- *Autumn* Ripe fruit, crops and vegetables are harvested.
- *Clouds* The sun warms the sea, lakes and rivers and water droplets escape into the sky where they are cooled forming a cloud. (*See* also Chapter 5 page 111.)
- *Wind* is the movement of air caused by warm air rising. Look at the movement of parachutes and kites in the wind; blow through a straw, blow 'out' a matchbox, or blow up balloons.

- *Rain, snow and sleet* fall from the clouds. When water droplets get too big and heavy they fall as rain or if the air is very
  cold it freezes them in the clouds and they then fall as ice
  particles.
- *Thunder* Electricity builds up in a cloud and then flashes to
  the ground or to another cloud creating lightning and crash-
  ing thunder from sound waves caused by heated air from the
  lightning which then contracts.
- *Variations* Your child can write down in his diary how the
  weather changes over a period of days. Explain how days
  shorten through the winter-time.

Reference
Catherall, Ed., *Exploring Weather*, Wayland 1990
Rogers, Daniel, *Weather*, Cherrytree Books 1989
Usborne *Spotter's Guides: The Weather*

Starting and Stopping
This is a simple investigation of *forces*. To show how a force can
be stored and turned into movement make a cotton-reel tank.
Then wind up the elastic band and off it goes!

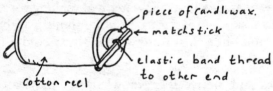

piece of candlewax.

matchstick

elastic band thread
to other end

cotton reel

Show how much easier it is to pull a book over pencils or
marbles than it is over the carpet alone. This illustrates the
presence of *frictional* force caused when things touch each other.

Flick a coin at a row of coins to see what happens. The 'force'
is transmitted through the row of coins and moves the last one.

The dangers of electricity
Explain that mains electricity can kill so power points, electric
wires and electric heaters must not be played with. Despite this it
is a convenient source of power – it makes things move, and it
makes light and heat.

Magnets Buy two magnets from a toy shop and ask your child to investigate what happens with a variety of objects such as pins, paper-clips, coins, hair grips etc.

Sounds
- Explain how sounds are produced by stringed instruments and percussion (vibrating object − − −→ air vibrations).
- Let him listen to a sea shell. The echoing sound waves within the cave-like interior of the shell sound like the breaking of waves on the beach.
- Where does the sound of the television come from? Radio waves bring sound from the television station to the television set. These are invisible waves and travel at the speed of light.

Colours, light and dark Light is made up of colours (which can be seen in the rainbow). The colours forming a ray of light are violet, indigo, blue, green, yellow, orange and red. Where there is no light, there is dark and shadows. At night the sun's light does not reach us so it is dark.

Biggest to smallest
The *Guinness Book of Records* illustrates a fascinating way to teach variation. Children are interested in the biggest things (dinosaurs, whales, giants), the fiercest (sharks, tigers) and the fastest (cheetah). Here are some that might appeal:

Biggest to smallest	*Fastest to slowest*	
Redwood tree	Hawk	100 mph
Blue whale	Cheetah	60 mph
Elephant	Man	20 mph
Horse	Mouse	5 mph
Dog	Snail	too slow to measure
Mouse		
Fly		

Other lists your child could make up could be 'heaviest to lightest', 'tallest to shortest', 'strongest to weakest'.

References
McFarlene, D., Ed., *Guinness Book of Records*, Guinness 1990
Usborne *Spotter's Guides: Dinosaurs*; *Fishes*
Usborne *Mysteries and Marvels* series

GRADED TESTS
FOR 5 TO 7 YEAR OLDS

ENGLISH

TEST 1

(1) Read aloud and then **copy the letters of the alphabet:**
(**Note to parent:** your child must also say the letters
phonically.)

a b c d e f g h i j k
l m n o p q r s t u v
w x y z

A B C D E F G H I
J K L M N O P Q R
S T U V W X Y Z

(2) **Read these words:** bus-stop, exit, danger, police

TEST 2

(1) **Write your name and address here:**

(2) **What do these words say?**

a and the he I in

is to of was that

(3) **Put the right word under the pictures:**

man   cat   jam   dots   dog   ten   leg   pin
pig   gun   cup

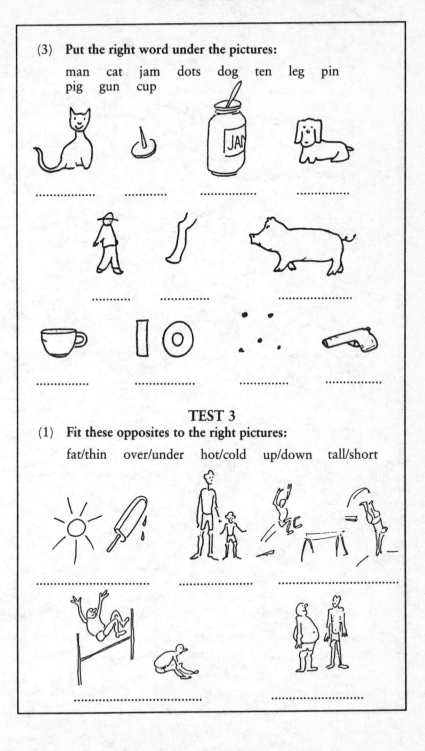

....

....

....

TEST 3

(1) **Fit these opposites to the right pictures:**

fat/thin   over/under   hot/cold   up/down   tall/short

....

....

(2) **Put the right words under these pictures:**

run tap dad bed hat top pen bag
dig pan nut

....

....

....

....

....

....

....

....

....

....

....

TEST 4

(1) **Read these words:**

as at be but all my go on are
for had have him his hot one
said went see some so they we
with you

(2)   **Put the right words under these pictures:**

room   boot   food   feet   ship   shop

....

....

(3)   **Fit these opposites with the right pictures:**

far/near   wide/narrow   more/less   push/pull

....

....

....

TEST 5

Fit these words to the right labels on the boy:

eye nose mouth hair arm hand
leg foot shoulder knee ankle elbow
chest stomach

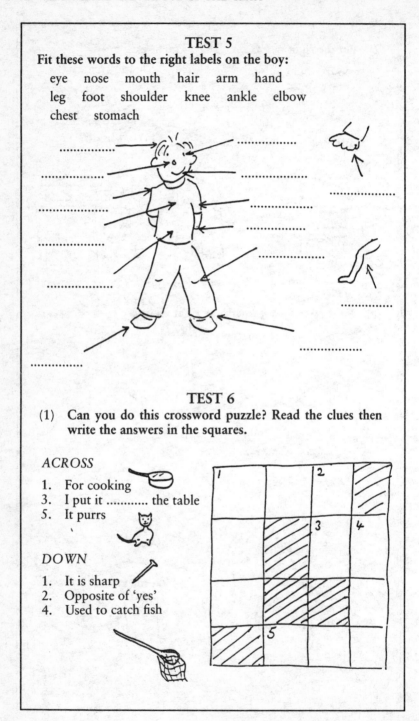

TEST 6

(1) **Can you do this crossword puzzle? Read the clues then write the answers in the squares.**

ACROSS

1. For cooking
3. I put it .... the table
5. It purrs

DOWN

1. It is sharp
2. Opposite of 'yes'
4. Used to catch fish

(2) **Can you label these objects from your home?**

vase   fork   knife   table   chair
cup   door   picture   brush   curtain   jug
spoon   television

....

....

....

....

TEST 7

(1) **Write the days of the week in order, starting with Sunday:**

Tuesday   Monday   Saturday   Thursday
Sunday   Friday   Wednesday

....

....

(2)   **Put the right word under each picture.**

car   flower   gate   lamp-post   tree   train   fly
grass   glove   swing   crown   bridge   cloud

....

....

....

....

....

MATHEMATICS

TEST 1

Note to parent: you may have to explain to your child what he has to do. He must know and understand the meaning of written numbers before doing the counting.

1   2   3   4   5   6   7   8   9   10

Count these:

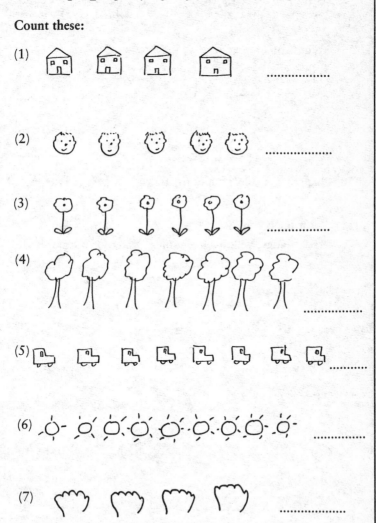

(8) **Copy these shapes:**

(**Note to parent:** Your child may need to trace over a shape with a pencil first.)

colour blue   colour yellow   colour red   colour orange

(9) **What comes next?**

....

....

(10) **Separate a pile of spoons, forks and knives into three sets.**

(11) **Spot the colours:**

red, orange, yellow, green, blue, violet (or purple).

TEST 2

1   2   3   4   5   6   7   8   9   10

11   12   13   14   15

Count these:

(1) ....

(2) ....

(3) ....

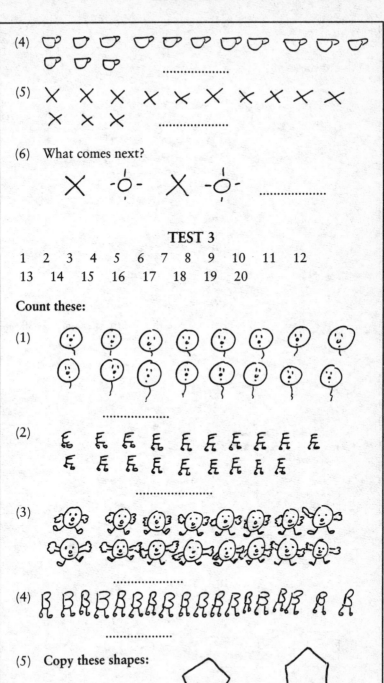

(4) ....

(5) ....

(6) What comes next?   ....

TEST 3

1   2   3   4   5   6   7   8   9   10   11   12
13   14   15   16   17   18   19   20

Count these:

(1) ....

(2) ....

(3) ....

(4) ....

(5) Copy these shapes:

TEST 4

Count these:

(1)

....

(2) 1 + 1 =   (7) 1 + 3 =

(3) 2 + 2 =   (8) 2 + 3 =

(4) 2 + 1 =   (9) 3 + 2 =

(5) 3 + 1 =   (10) 3 + 1 =

(6) 1 + 2 =   (11) **Write the numbers from 1 to 30**

TEST 5

Can you do these sums?

(1) 3 + 3 =   (6) 4 + 2 =

(2) 3 + 4 =   (7) 5 + 1 =

(3) 4 + 1 =   (8) 1 + 5 =

(4) 1 + 4 =   (9) 6 + 2 =

(5) 2 + 4 =   (10) 2 + 6 =

(11) **What are the names of these shapes?**

....

TEST 6

How many is this?

(1) 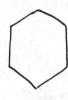 = Tens (t)   Units (u)

(2) 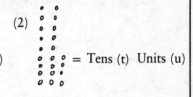 = Tens (t) Units (u)

(3) **What are these called?**

....

(**Note to parent:** some children of this age cannot see in 3-D. You may need to produce a *real* cube.)

Take away:

(Example: 4 − 1 = 3)

(4) 3 🚚 🚚 🚚 − 1 = ...

(5) 5 😊 😊 😊 😊 😊 − 2 = ...

(6) 5 🐞 🐞 🐞 🐞 🐞 − 3 = ...

(7) **Write the numbers from 1 to 50**

TEST 7

Can you do these sums?

(1) 4 + 6 = ... (5) 11 + 7 = ...

(2) 7 + 3 = ... (6) 6 − 2 = ...

(3) 8 + 4 = ... (7) 8 − 3 = ...

(4) 9 + 3 = ... (8) 9 − 5 = ...

(9) 1 + ☐ = 2   (10) ☐ + 2 = 3

If possible use a 100 bead abacus and count to:

(a) 20   (b) 30   (c) 40   (d) 70   (e) 90   (f) 54
(g) 67   (h) 79   (i) 100

TEST 8

(1) **Write as numbers:**

one   two   three   four   five

....

(2) **Write as words:**

1   2   3   4   5

....

(3) **Mark the biggest number:**

3   7   4   12

(4) Tens   Units   **What is this number?**

(5) Tens   Units   **What is this number?**

(6)   **Write the times under these clocks.**

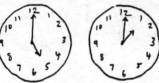

.... o'clock   ....o'clock   ....o'clock   ....o'clock

(7)   **What is the underlined number?**

(a) 2̲1   (b) 34̲   (c) 7̲7

....

(8)   **Mark the *even* numbers.**

1   3   4   7   6   12

TEST 9

How many pence?

(1) 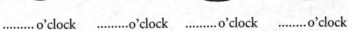 (1p) (1p) (1p) (1p) (1p) (1p) = ... p

(2) (2p) (1 p) (1p) (1p) = ... p

(3) (2p) (2p) (1p) = ... p

Use the number line to do these sums:

(4)   3 + 8   = ...

(5)   8 + 3   = ...

(6)   10 + 5   = ...

(7)   5 + 10   = ...

(8)   8   (9)   7   (10)   8   (11)   12
     + 6   + 4   − 3   − 7
   _____   _____   _____   _____

(12)   **Fill in the gaps:**

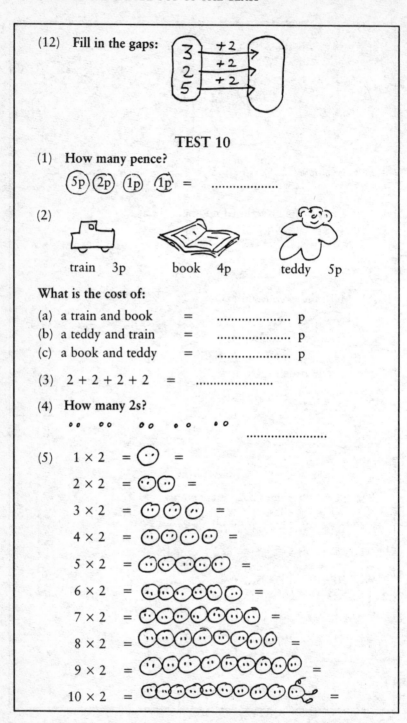

TEST 10

(1)   **How many pence?**

(5p) (2p) (1p) (1p) = ...

(2)

train   3p   book   4p   teddy   5p

What is the cost of:

(a)   a train and book   = ... p
(b)   a teddy and train   = ... p
(c)   a book and teddy   = ... p

(3) $2 + 2 + 2 + 2$ = ...

(4)   **How many 2s?**

°°   °°   °°   °°   °°

....

(5) 1×2 = ⊙ =

2×2 = ⊙⊙ =

3×2 = ⊙⊙⊙ =

4×2 = ⊙⊙⊙⊙ =

5×2 = ⊙⊙⊙⊙⊙ =

6×2 = ⊙⊙⊙⊙⊙⊙ =

7×2 = ⊙⊙⊙⊙⊙⊙⊙ =

8×2 = ⊙⊙⊙⊙⊙⊙⊙⊙ =

9×2 = ⊙⊙⊙⊙⊙⊙⊙⊙⊙ =

10×2 = ⊙⊙⊙⊙⊙⊙⊙⊙⊙⊙ =

(6) What shape is this?

....

(7) What fraction is the shaded part?

....

(8) Mark the *odd* numbers:

2   1   4   6   3   5

(9) What is 2 *more* than 4? ....

(Note to parent: the number line or practical objects may be useful.)

(10) What is the *difference* between 5 and 3? ....

TEST 11

How many pence?

(1) (10p) (2p) (1p)(1p)(1p) = ... p

(2) (10p) (5p) (1p) = ...p

(3) What is the change from 5p when buying each of these?

train   1p   book 2p   teddy   3p

....

(Note to parent: use real or plastic coins.)

(4)   **Continue the patterns:**

    (a)   2   4   6   ....

    (b)   10   20   30   ....

(5)   **Count in 5s:**

    5   10   15   20   25   30   35
    40   45   50

(6)   **What fraction is the shaded part in each picture?**

(a)   (b)

....

TEST 12

(1)   **Share these sweets between 2 people:**

How many does each one get?   ....

(**Note to parent:** best shown *practically.*)

(2)   **Share these between 2 people:**

How many does each one get?   ....

Write in the correct number of dots.

(3) 5 × 2 = ⭕⭕⭕⭕⭕ = ...

(4) 7 × 2 = ⭕⭕⭕⭕⭕⭕⭕ = ...

(5) ice-cream

lolly

  (a) **How many men like ice-cream?** ....

  (b) **How many like lollies?** ....

(6) **Draw the lines of symmetry in the capital letters of the alphabet:**

A B C D E F G H I
J K L M N O P Q R
S T U V W X Y Z

CHAPTER FIVE

YOUR CHILD FROM SEVEN TO NINE

At this stage there seems to be a sudden spurt of interest in times past, although a child is muddled over whether or not Nelson or George Washington are mentioned in the Bible. By 9 he can use the telephone well, find out and decide what programmes he wants to watch on television, is extremely competent at computer game videos but is unable to repeat his school timetable of subjects. For him to be happy doing a task, he needs to be told how much there is to do and how long it will take.

Your child is also beginning to recognise various aspects of world relationships, and be interested in foreign countries. He is adventurous, daring to trespass into neighbours' gardens from time to time. By 8 years of age, a child can use spoken language as fluently as an adult. He finds stories and poems in which adults (especially teachers) are made a fool of extremely funny. He can also verbalise ideas and problems.

Attitudes

Now that your child's first flush of interest in schoolwork has worn off his attitude to learning will have become apparent. Some children need very firm guidance in what they should do, others are happier discovering more for themselves. Susan was in the former category: at school, in a formal setting, she was very content. Later, when she moved to a school where no firm objectives were given to her ('the children learn by osmosis', said one parent), she became morose and depressed at home. In one year her reading age fell back by 18 months. 'I wish they would *give* me something to do,' she said. 'The other children just talk and play around all day.' Her brother, Chris, was the opposite. He hated being directed too firmly. As long as he was given reasonable objectives he was happy to find his own pathway to learning success. In between these extremes are many who like some direction in learning and some freedom. And there are always those who would prefer to play football or computer games interminably. There are children who like painting and there are children who loathe painting. In one class, when a teacher said to the 8-year-olds, 'Get out your handwriting books', all the girls said 'Goodee', and all the boys groaned.

Attainment
There is a wide range of attainment, too. John at 8 was a whiz at calculus. Many children are still not competent at adding and subtracting. Sometimes, parents have taught tables at home. Alan was one of these. He proudly showed me his battered tables book. 'I can do up to the Twenty Times table,' he said. He certainly could. He was brilliant at times sums, but could not figure out his change at the shop. His Maths development was lopsided and he could not read or spell very well.

The Energetic Age
First Year Juniors, in particular, still retain a lot of their infant enthusiasm and 'bounce', and this readily transfers into work. Mark often has to be *made* to stop doing his Maths and English work-book in order to go to bed.

However, because they have put so much energy into their day, this age often tire quickly as the evening wears on. After about 8.30 p.m. most are too tired to concentrate on anything academic. One Moslem boy I know of breaks the mould, however. Straight after school he goes to the Mosque to learn for two hours, then to a house to pray for an additional hour, and after that does schoolwork for another hour. He has his tea at 8.15 p.m.! Yet he is one of the liveliest and happiest boys I know.

Encouragement and Failure

Young children have not yet come to terms with failure and it is necessary to point out that, 'Everybody finds this difficult', or 'Perhaps *this* is easier for some but you found that other subject much easier than others do'. Some subjects are difficult for all children until they are facile. Fractions are difficult, division is difficult, and problems most certainly tax the most. It is extremely important that a child understands that others also find things difficult. In a classroom she may not always get this impression. Sometimes it seems to her that everybody else understands everything. If she struggles she must know that it is to be expected because 'everybody struggles here'. Of course, many adults also have difficulty with failure, probably stemming from this time in their childhood.

Peter is going through this phase at the moment. At 8, he feels that he must know about everything put in front of him. 'I can do *all* this,' he says, hardly glancing at the work. When he can't do something he gets angry. His mother has to explain to him, 'It doesn't matter if you can't do it. Lots of children can't. It's just something we will have to teach you. You are clever and will learn about it very quickly.'

Problems, Problems

Worded examples appear in Maths books for this age and they certainly accelerate the development of 'intelligence'. The wide ranging use of skills and strategies necessary to solve a variety of problems, both theoretical and practical, increases a general ability to think and seems to give more confidence. If you exercise the mind it grows 'fatter' in response, the better to cope with more strenuous demands in the future.

As in other areas, there are vast differences in children. Helen could figure out problems by herself after knowing basic number work. Claire had to persist and persist until she found a solution, often with an adult sitting alongside giving encouragement, showing her how to abstract a sum from words. Difficulties with problem solving can be crystallised as being due to one of the following:

(1) Being used to substituting 'rules' for understanding in the past and having insufficient grounding in concepts.

(2) Difficulties in understanding words or symbols in the problem, and difficulties in comprehending the overall meaning of a sentence.

(3) Difficulty in breaking down a problem into its elements, and setting it down badly on paper so that links cannot be established with memory. Clear presentation of constituent sums on paper can often lead to mental images being linked and understanding being effected more quickly. A problem like 'I go to the shop and buy two things which cost 3p and 2p. How much change have I?' can be written down on paper as:

I have   10p

The two things cost 2p + 3p   =   5p

The change I have is 10p
                                    −5p
                                    ‾‾‾‾
                                      5p
                                    ‾‾‾‾

The link to establish in the child's mind, through a mental image, is that difference between 10 and 5. The taking-away sum is simply an operation to facilitate the complete solution. The complete mental process involved here would be:

I have 10 → bigger →
I lose 5   → smaller → I have some left over

Therefore, the child should write down the subtraction sum, unless she can count clearly in her mind.

Helping not hindering

Beware that your child is not manipulating you. Robert spent half his time using his intelligence in trying to get *me* to do his problems for him. After all, had he not tried it out on his teacher at school and found that it worked every time? Here then is a common snare for a parent tutor: the child learns that if she closes her mind to a problem, eventually someone will step in to do it for her. This, incidentally, poses a problem for psychological testing. A child will not always respond to her maximum potential, particularly if the tester is a stranger. At 2 years and 10 months, John read like a 7-year-old, could count well and tell the time. An educational psychologist came to the house to test him but John would do virtually nothing. At the end of a testing session the psychologist pronounced that, 'Your child is average. You have nothing to worry about.' The performance was affected by nervousness, but many children deliberately 'play dumb' and get very upset when found out. Ruth behaved so and a little later, when I was still waiting for her answer she told me, 'But I really don't know how to do this! My teacher *always* tells me the answer!' Then, when I suggested that she was tricking me, she knew that the game was up! After that, she began to perform as I knew she could and she concentrated more and more. Children who resort to kidding adults into always giving them the answer eventually lose confidence in themselves; they come to believe that they really do not have the brain power to work things out for themselves. The strategies a child adopts at 7 or 8 may determine whether or not she succeeds throughout her academic life.

Somehow, in the work that you give your child at home, you will have to strike a balance between explaining things fully and leaving some of the thinking to her. Should you leave her thinking about a problem for 10 minutes? Is he too tired to think? Is he 'trying something on' with you so that he controls the action? Or, maybe, he just does not understand. These are fundamental problems that a parent teacher must wrestle with. A parent believes in her child's largely untapped ability to perform far beyond what others believe is possible and she must ensure that a child reaches deep into her own resources for answers. She also needs to ensure that the language and fundamental elements of a task are understood. A parent is certainly in the best position to really know her child, whereas a teacher working with 30 or more children in a noisy, busy classroom has little hope of doing so.

ENGLISH: READING

Most children can read quite well by 7 and 8. Many who cannot simply need personal attention in their reading (unless they have severe physical or mental defects). One child of 7 who could not read a single word after two years at school learnt to read after his father and I sat down with him for half an hour a day. We used Look and Say methods, Key Words and phonics. When his father took him to school after only a few weeks and showed them that he could read quite well, the headmaster said, 'It's a miracle!' It was certainly no miracle. I have helped many such backward readers to get started: they needed only daily attention and clear presentation of words. When they could read well all these children were overjoyed. They told absolutely *everybody*!

Books

Children tend to consolidate their reading with easy reading books which have humour and adventure. This explains the popularity of Enid Blyton, frowned on by supporters of 'high' literature, but excellent books to encourage an interest in reading. Some are a little dated but they tend to lead children on to 'better' books.

Early Reading

Here are some more books to add to the list already given:

Ahlberg, Allan, *Woof!*, Viking Kestrel 1986

Blume, Judy, *Superfudge*, The Bodley Head 1980

Blyton, Enid, *Famous Five* books, Hodder & Stoughton; *Secret Seven* books, Hodder & Stoughton

Dahl, Roald, *The B.F.G.*, Cape 1982; *Danny The Champion of the World*, Cape 1975

Ireson, Barbara, Ed., *Book of Verse*, Penguin 1970

Opie, Iona and Peter, Ed., *The Oxford Book of Children's Verse*, Oxford University Press 1973

Better Readers

Crompton, Richmal, *Just William* books, Macmillan

Dahl, Roald, *Revolting Rhymes*, Cape 1982

Lewis, C.S., *The Lion, the Witch and the Wardrobe*, Collins 1974

Serraillier, Ian, *The Silver Sword*, Cape 1956

Spelling

Some bad spellers are also poor readers. Helen (age 9) and her
older sister, on the other hand, have great difficulty with spelling
although they are good readers. Somewhere along the line they
had not learnt to sound out 'hard' consonants (b, d, etc.)
properly when writing them down. They also experienced difficulty in distinguishing short vowel sounds, a problem I encounter constantly with much younger children. Laura did not learn
to spell well until she was at her Secondary School when a wise
teacher gave the class spellings to learn every week and also
asked them to use them in their writing.

After a child has mastered the use of short vowel and consonant sounds and double-letter word beginnings as detailed in the
previous chapter, she can follow on by learning long vowel
sounds and building double and triple syllable words. Where a
syllable or word does not fit in to the phonic scheme it can be
visualised as an 'oddity'. Such 'oddities' occur most often in the
middle of words, and word middles cause more trouble than
word beginnings and word endings.

Determination This can be learnt by getting a child to remember
constituent syllables through visualising and sounding them out,
and then writing down the whole word, noting oddities:

> de   — phonic
> -ter   — phonic
> -min — phonic
> a-   — phonic (long vowel)
> -tion — 'oddity', said 'shon' or 'shun'

Picturing oddities is an excellent way of remembering spellings. I
can remember as a child being fascinated by a *buoy* bobbing in
the bay, and by the fact that it was not a real *boy* out there. I
tossed around the idea of 'boy' versus 'buoy' and their spelling
and meaning for literally hours.

The grouping of words of similar strings of letters gives a
sense of the position in words and the frequency of such strings,
for example, q always has u with it, c and k often appear
together, and t, c, and h are often combined at word ends (for
example, hatch, catch).

Silent letters can also be introduced at this stage. These are oddities, especially the silent **b**, most easily recognised by many children. Words with silent letters can be visualised with the silent letter departing for a while, and then returning to 'hover' over its position for a time:

Homophones are words of different meaning but pronounced alike. These should be learnt in conjunction with their meanings and this is best done in association with pictures or in writing stories and diaries.

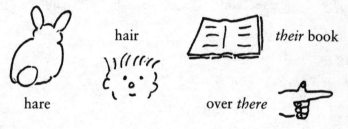

hair

their book

hare

over *there*

Long vowels

able   we   ice   no   unit

radio   even   island   go   usual

Blends and silent letters

sea   eat   leaf

see

sing   ring   fling   king

head   bread   dead

boat   soap   road

when   why   who   where   what

cry   fly   try   shy

happy   mummy   silly   daddy   (after double letters)

coin   join

boy   toy

rain   train   sail

day   say   play

out   shout   cloud

how   down   clown

lamb   climb   thumb

hour   ghost   rhyme

fight   sight   light   night   fright   bright   tonight

right

know   knee   knife

write   wrist   wrong

hair   fair   chair   pair

bar   card   hard   dark

ear   hear   clear   bear   wear   pear   tear

bird   first   girl   birthday

burn   hurt   church   purse

drawer   paw   saw   claw

few   chew   crew

low   show   grow

work   word   world

back   sock   lock   neck

catch   latch   fetch

bell   hill   shell

pass hiss glass cross

splash split

spring spray

queen quick quarter

blue true glue

square squeak

toe goes tomatoes potatoes

earth heard early

piece field chief

our hour flour

flower

talked pulled mended shouted

try tried

cry cried

berry berries

poor door floor

many any

wash want watch

sure cure

four your pour

sauce Santa Claus

Reference

Schonell, Frederick J., *Essential Read-Spell series*, Macmillan 1977/83; *Essential Spelling List*, Macmillan 1932; *Essentials in Teaching and Testing*, Macmillan 1985

ENGLISH: WRITING

There are several forms of writing: letters, diaries, reports of investigations, non-fiction and creative writing. The latter category causes teachers and tutors most difficulty. Children asked to write from their own experience quite often cannot recall anything of significance in their life to set down on paper. Your child will need stimulation to write and such motivation can come from a variety of sources:

(1)   *From their own experience* A football match. A school trip. I'm frightened of the dark. What happened in my favourite television programme. My hobby. My birthday party. What I like and what I don't like. Christmas. My holiday.

(2)   *Story titles* If I turned into a Giant. The Haunted House. My Pet is a Dragon. My dinosaur can do that. Adventure under the Sea. The Boy who wanted to be King. My Invisible Friend. The Magic Chocolates. My teacher is an Alien. How Robert saved the World.

(3)   *Pieces from stories* Read your child a paragraph from a book to start a story or to give an ending to work towards. Writing about stories that they know, or about a video they have seen, is very productive. Once a child has a clear visual image of a story she finds it easier to transfer to paper. Disney fairy-tale cartoons are good resource material.

(4)   *Music* Pieces like 'Mars, the bringer of war' by Holst seem to conjure up very vivid pictures in children's minds: of giants, witches, and dark deeds.

(5)   *Groups of words* Ask your child to make a short story from a group of words. For example:

(a) boy, dog, storm, castle, witch, magic ring, home
(b) girl, boat, storm, island, forest, tiger, palace, king, home

Your child can be told that she need not include every word. They are merely 'guide' words.

(6)   *Groups of sentences* Make a story from them: The boy was lost. The fog was very thick. He heard a roaring noise. As he ran away, his foot slipped. He climbed higher and higher. His heart beat faster and faster.

(7) *Writing factual information* Some of this can be put into story form: dinosaurs, African animals, pets, sharks, whales, the moon, space travel, castles, the jungle, mountains, desert islands, the Frozen North, deserts.

(8) *Reading helps writing* Children get ideas from the books they read, they learn new words and they learn from the style of the author. As I have already noted the poorest writers are often the poorest readers. Today television often seems to take precedence over reading, especially among boys.

(9) *Typing a story* Your child may be stimulated if he can type a story, either on the typewriter or at the computer keyboard.

Strategies for helping your child's writing

Philip is 12 now. At 10, his teacher said, 'He is far behind the class in word knowledge. His writing is poor.' However, he was brilliant at spelling, could punctuate well and had a keen mind (he had also read widely from a young age). After he had been shown how to express himself by the better use of words, well-constructed sentences and the use of more 'colourful' ideas, he improved rapidly. In six months he wrote a marvellous short piece and came top out of one thousand in a Grammar School Entrance Examination.

Too many children are encouraged to throw something, anything, on to the page. That is part of them, it is reasoned, so it must be good. This is not necessarily so. As long as the creative flair within a child is not hampered by excessive correction, the acquisition of an increasing range of skills (use of alternative words, better sentences and ideas, and improved plot structure) will only serve to improve the child's written expression of her innermost thoughts.

Strategies in helping your child's writing are:

(1) Improving his stock of word meanings. This comes from reading and also from exercises (e.g. opposites). Your child should realise that the presence or absence of a word should be thought about carefully. A word like 'nice' and repetitions like 'and then' could certainly be replaced.

(2) The sentence is the basic unit of writing. A writer must learn that a sentence needs to be worked on and before she

writes it out she should ask herself, 'Is this the best sentence I could write?'

(3)   A child should be encouraged to use her senses in description. In describing a room she could mention, for example, the colour of the carpets, noise from the television, two people talking, the banging of a door, the texture of curtains, the smell of cooking, or the taste of a beefburger eaten at the table.

Movement is important (I ran upstairs two at a time) as is a sense of time (my teddy bear is in the corner. I had it when I was very small).

(4)   Your child should write notes before writing a story – a beginning, a middle (the major part), and an ending. She should visualise the story from beginning to end and make events in it significant and exciting or humorous. Conflict makes for a good story too especially 'baddies' versus 'goodies'.

Little Red Riding Hood has all the elements of a good story. It introduces the characters briefly, there is conflict – the wolf wants to eat Red Riding Hood but she wishes to live for a few more years yet. The story builds up to a climax in her Grandmother's house and the conflict is resolved. The wolf is killed and they all live happily ever after.

(5)   Writing need not, of course, be a dramatic story. Some children learn quickly, from poetry and certain authors, to write down their own feelings in a piece. However, style is important. Description should appeal to the senses and dialogue should contain colour and conflict.

Punctuation

The sentence is very important. Children should understand the meaning of a full stop and be aware of the use of capital letters. Exercises teach this, but a certain amount of correction of prose is necessary.

Capitals

- These occur at the beginnings of sentences.
- They are used for proper nouns — names, places, months, days, book titles, etc.

Word Meanings

These can be taught through reading, through finding opposites, by inserting words into 'gaps' left in sentences, and through homophones.

Opposites These are best learnt by visualisation. For example: 'sad/happy', these are easy to visualise while 'bought/sold' are more difficult.

Useful words for 8-year-olds to use in writing

birthday   grandma   yesterday   picture   because

aeroplane   television   brought   tomorrow   morning

afternoon   wood   bonfire   rocket   colour   football

castle   elephant   sometimes   dinosaur   whale   shark

pretty   firework   church   through   queen   catch

cry   cried   hospital   breakfast   fair   doctor   bicycle

please   animal   knock   magic   ready   wheel   grass

orange   chocolate   caught   build   eight   monkey

pair   write   something   clean   head   garage   teacher

engine   won   snowman   bread   kitten   harvest

piece   cousin   chair   balloon   change   together

picnic   front   mouse   decorate   prince   snowball

donkey   soldier   princess   nurse   favour   laugh

pencil   die   mountain   horse

MATHEMATICS

Counting on and on

A knowledge of large numbers and their approximations is becoming increasingly important in Mathematics. It is also important that a child is aware of place value (e.g. that the 5 in 542 means 500).

Your child should now be at the stage where he is aware of tens and units. Setting down numbers in the honoured fashion of tens and units is very effective in teaching place value and is invaluable in pointing out the extension into decimals:

Tens (t)	Units (u)
5	2

Number patterns If a square *array* of numbers is set out on paper this can help a child with sums especially multiplication as it presents many opportunities to discover number patterns. A certain amount of practice with numbers should extend learning with these up to 1000:

	1	2	3	4	5	6	7	8	9	10
×10										
×100	→10	20	30	40	50	60	70	80	90	100
×10										
	→ 100	200	300	400	500	600	700	800	900	1000

This array should extend numbers into, for example:

Hundreds	Tens	Units			
5	3	6	(5	=	500)

Addition arrays are also valuable:

1	2	3	4	5	6	7	8	9	10
11	12	13	14	15	16	17	18	19	20
21	22	23	24	25	26	27	28	29	30
31	32	33	34	35	36	37	38	39	40
41	42	43	44	45	46	47	48	49	50
51	52	53	54	55	56	57	58	59	60
61	62	63	64	65	66	67	68	69	70
71	72	73	74	75	76	77	78	79	80
81	82	83	84	85	86	87	88	89	90
91	92	93	94	95	96	97	98	99	100

Used in conjunction with a 10×10 abacus this array shows clearly that $2 + 10 = 12$ or $67 + 10 = 77$.

The difficulty with Maths is that all too soon children can learn to 'think' in processes, which is understanding at a superficial level. Whole networks of schemata can then be built up by linking into memory new schemata, without reference to deeper meaning. This is understandable because every time a child does a sum he cannot refer back to real life. For 365 + 763 only has deeper meaning if 365 marbles can be seen joining forces with 763 marbles. This 'skimming' for meaning is an essential part of everyday life but it is necessary to give at least a *sense* of deeper meaning, and arrays assist in this.

If practice with bigger numbers is not effected, difficulties arise, particularly in problem solving. Philip, at 11, had difficulty visualising numbers bigger than 12 (he went abroad for 2 years when he was 6 and missed out on consolidation work).

He was very capable at processes like 237 + 456 = 693, but could not visualise 'What is 3 more than 26?', although he instantly had the answer to 'What is 5 more than 4?' Some problem solving techniques are better taught by using numbers smaller than 10 because of the difficulty some children have in thinking in larger numbers.

Using an array for table learning
In an array a pattern can be spotted. This can be seen here in the Two Times and Five Times tables. And also below in the Five and Ten Times Tables square array.

Two Times table:

1 (2) 3 (4) 5 (6) 7 (8) 9 (10)

Five Times table:

1 2 3 4 (5) 6 7 8 9 (10)

The Five Times and Ten Times Tables Array

1	2	3	4	(5)	6	7	8	9	(10)
11	12	13	14	(15)	16	17	18	19	(20)
21	22	23	24	(25)	26	27	28	29	(30)
31	32	33	34	(35)	36	37	38	39	(40)
41	42	43	44	(45)	46	47	48	49	(50)
51	52	53	54	(55)	56	57	58	59	(60)
61	62	63	64	(65)	66	67	68	69	(70)
71	72	73	74	(75)	76	77	78	79	(80)
81	82	83	84	(85)	86	87	88	89	(90)
91	92	93	94	(95)	96	97	98	99	(100)

The Five Times Table	The Ten Times Table
$1 \times 5 = 5$	$1 \times 10 = 10$
$2 \times 5 = 10$	$2 \times 10 = 20$
$3 \times 5 = 15$	$3 \times 10 = 30$
$4 \times 5 = 20$	$4 \times 10 = 40$
$5 \times 5 = 25$	$5 \times 10 = 50$
$6 \times 5 = 30$	$6 \times 10 = 60$
$7 \times 5 = 35$	$7 \times 10 = 70$
$8 \times 5 = 40$	$8 \times 10 = 80$
$9 \times 5 = 45$	$9 \times 10 = 90$
$10 \times 5 = 50$	$10 \times 10 = 100$

Children need to know at least their Two Times, Five Times and Ten Times tables by 8 or 9. Using symbols as on page 46 is still an effective way of learning tables.

The Clock and Time

It is necessary to reinforce the ideas of minutes *past* and minutes *to* (*see* page 49). Teach your child minutes past first and when he is sure of this, only then move on to minutes to (counting back). Knowing the Five Times table is useful because then he can count quickly on the clock numbers.

An additional complication to explain is that times are written as 2.38 as well as 22 minutes to.

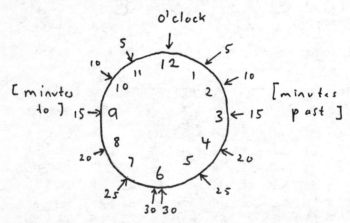

The passing of time Start by working within a single hour. Your child will need to know that 10.50 is later than 10.35 by 15 minutes.

The Time Line

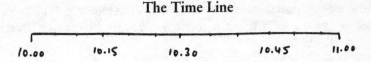

Further addition and subtraction

Using the 100 array This is useful for a while to show 32 + 10, 32 + 5, 17 + 11 and so on but the time comes when progress is quicker if a child is shown addition and subtraction in a more formal way. Keep referring back to the abacus and array though, because although formal sums represent a useful process, consolidation of understanding is still necessary.

Tens	Units		Tens	Units
(t)	(u)		(t)	(u)
2	1		7	3
+ 3	4		− 4	1
5	5		3	2

↖ start from this side   ↖ start from this side

Children instinctively start sums with the left-hand row first because they read from left to right.

Carrying and borrowing To emphasise the carrying process, cut out several strips of card and mark them off into 10 pieces. These are 'tens'. One of these strips cut up into the constituent pieces gives the 'units'.

Tens	Units
(t)	(u)
2	7
+ 1	4
4	1

→

Tens (t)

+

Showing this practical operation is very effective in giving meaning to the sum. Similarly, borrowing can be demonstrated
practically:

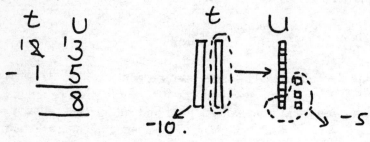

Later the practical side can be shown.

$$
\begin{array}{cc}
t & u \\
2 & 4 \\
+\ 1 & 6 \\
\hline
4 & \textcircled{1}0 \\
1 &
\end{array}
\qquad
\begin{array}{cc}
t & u \\
\not{1}\,2 & \overset{10+}{\not{4}}\,1 \\
-\ 1 & 3 \\
\hline
& 8
\end{array}
$$

Money

This is best dealt with practically. Extend the concept of
shopping and counting to include parts of £1.00:

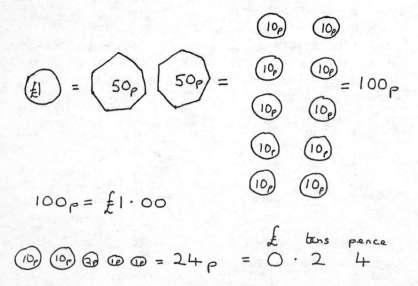

$100p = £1 \cdot 00$

Considerable practice is necessary to establish the connection between the decimal representation and real-life sums.

Shopping sums
Adding items: A book costs 64p and a toy 27p.

	£	tens	pence
	0 .	6	4
+	0 .	2	7
	0 .	9	1

Change: Calculating change is a difficult step for a child because it incorporates two basic sums – adding the cost of items and subtracting to work out the change. These elements should be clearly separated:

Cost   teddy 25p, books 15p. *I have 50p.*

	£	tens	pence		
	0 .	2	5		
+	0 .	1	5		
	0 .	4	0	cost	40p

Change

	£	tens	pence		
	0 .	5	0		
−	0 .	4	0		
	0 .	1	0	change	10p

Children should be encouraged to write down sums and not carry them in their head. Doing so is effectively extending practice, for images are liable to being displaced by other sensory input.

Later, confusion arises because 'units' here occur in the place where hundredths are written. Try to emphasise that £1 is 100p.

Extension of multiplication and division

Until a child is familiar with the mechanisms both multiplication and division are best extended by using the Two Times table. I show the order in which the working out should be done in the sum.

Sometimes, great satisfaction is expressed when a child feels he has mastered a manipulative skill. 'I can do it! I can do it!' shouted Philip, aged 7, jumping up and down and spilling his drink of 'pop'. Further extension into multiplication involves carrying.

Similarly, small numbers should be used for division:

Say, 'How many 2s in 6?' This needs much practice. There is a tendency to say 2×6 and give the answer 12. Also practise with $6 \div 2 = 3$.

Remainders This can be shown by sharing 5 sweets between 2 people.

Step 1

Step 2

$$2\overline{)5}\text{2 remainder 1}$$

Both these practical and simple abstract steps need consolidation before the introduction of Step 3 below.

Step 3

$$2\overline{)3\,{}^{1}2}16$$

Measurement

Length Of the three concepts length, weight and volume, length is best understood by a child, probably because of more practical consolidation in school.

1000 metres (m)	=	1 kilometre (km)
100 centimetres (cm)	=	1 metre
10 millimetres (mm)	=	1 centimetre

One Metre

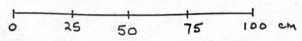

$\frac{1}{4}$ of 1 metre = 25 cm
$\frac{1}{2}$ of 1 metre = 50 cm
$\frac{3}{4}$ of 1 metre = 75 cm

One Kilometre

$^1/_4$ of 1 kilometre = 250 m
$^1/_2$ of 1 kilometre = 500 m
$^3/_4$ of 1 kilometre = 750 m

Weight

You should introduce your child to the idea of 100 grams (g) =
1 kilogram (kg). Allow her to weigh packets of food to check
their weights. She can see, for example, that ½ kg = 500g.
Adding up weights is a useful exercise.

	Hundreds	Tens	Units	
sugar	5	0	0	g
cereal	3	5	0	g
tin soup	4	0	0	g
total	12	5	0	g

	Thousands	Hundreds	Tens	Units	
total	1	2	5	0	g

This brings in the idea of hundreds and thousands. After considerable practice with the above you can introduce:

$$1250g \quad = \quad 1000g \quad + \quad 250g$$
$$= \quad 1 \text{ kg} \quad \text{and} \quad 250g$$

1 kilogram = 1000 g
$^1/_2$ of 1 kilogram = 500 g
$^1/_4$ of 1 kilogram = 250 g

Volume

Extension into writing down volumes measured in a graduated kitchen jug will help teach volume measures:

$$1000 \text{ ml } (\text{cm}^3) = 1 \text{ litre}$$
$$500 \text{ ml} \qquad = \tfrac{1}{2} \text{ litre}$$
$$250 \text{ ml} \qquad = \tfrac{1}{4} \text{ litre}$$

Explain that $\tfrac{1}{2}$ is 1 out of 2 or a half, and $\tfrac{1}{4}$ is 1 out of 4 or a quarter.

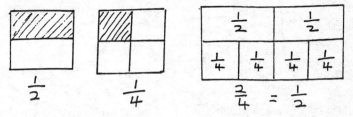

Estimations

Your child will need to be aware of which units to use for what distance, weight or volume, and also have a sense of the *meaning* of that distance, weight or volume when expressed in abstract units. In a world of computers it is necessary not to lose the capacity to estimate.

You can ask her questions that will probe her understanding. Such questions could be: How tall is a man? How high is a cloud? How long is my road? How far is it to town? How long is this book? How long is a rubber (eraser)? How heavy is a lorry? How much milk is there in a bottle? How much petrol is there in the petrol tank of a car?

Function Machines

Your child is bound to meet displays of the type:

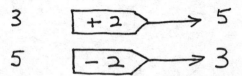

Sufficient practice with examples like this will demonstrate that subtraction is the reverse of addition.

Negative numbers and the temperature scale

Show your child that the thermometer does not stop at *zero*. Explain that when it is very cold the liquid in the thermometer goes below zero. This fascinates children. They ask, 'How cold can it get?' You discuss the Ice Age and how the dinosaurs became extinct.

Negative numbers

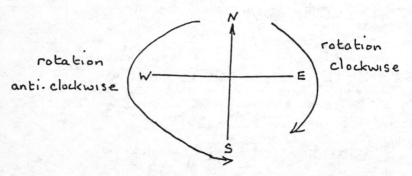

John was $3\frac{1}{2}$ years old when he learnt about negative numbers. He was fascinated and asked questions about them for weeks.

Area

Centimetre square paper or graph paper can be used to demonstrate area. Place an object on the paper and ask your child to draw round it. She can then count the number of squares the object covers (more than half a square counts as one whole one).

Rotation

Use the compass point as on page 54.

Your child can try moving through various angles (e.g. 180° clockwise, 270° anticlockwise – i.e. 2 × 90° and 3 × 90°).

Reflection

Let your child investigate how objects look in a mirror. The use of capital letters shows clearly that the image is reversed:

E   will be   Ǝ

Using the calculator and computer

In today's world children are taught to use these at an early age but they are used to supplement basic teaching. Children get much pleasure from working with technical aids.

The calculator A child gains great confidence from the use of a calculator. She can use it to check her sums. She can estimate an answer, for example 20 + 23, and check how close she was:

20 + 23 is about 20 + 20 = 40

The calculator says 43

Big numbers Children find it difficult to visualise hundreds and thousands. The calculator can help them with this:

$$100 + 100 + 100 + 100 + 100 + 100 + 100 + 100 + 100 + 100 = \underline{1000}$$

$$\text{or} \quad 10 \times 100 = \underline{1000}$$

Similar play can give an idea of the addition and multiplication of thousands.

Times 10, Times 100 Your child can discover for himself that $2 \times 10 = 20$ (2 with one nought attached) and $2 \times 100 = 200$ (2 with two noughts attached).

Computers These can be used to supplement the teaching of your child. There is much software (some listed in this book) which can help with early learning. It is a good idea to 'tie in' computer work at home with that at school. Therefore, it will be necessary to find out what computer the school uses, and also have an idea of what software is being used.

SCIENCE

Material sorting

Your child can investigate the physical properties of various materials or substances. He can use a scrapbook to draw pictures and write down any words that he wishes to use to describe the materials.

Materials: water, earth, paper, cloth, metal (iron or aluminium), plasticine, wood, plastic, rubber, glass (marbles), stone, etc.

Words to use when describing materials: shiny, soft, crinkly, crumpled, torn, smooth, rough, cold, warm, heavy, light, bendy, granules, black, silver, white, see-through, strong, weak, sharp, rounded, bouncy, stretch, squash, pour, liquid, solid, drip, dribble, runs, edge

Animal groups: Here are some ideas for groups for your child to investigate and write about: insects (6 legs), spiders (8 legs), crabs (hard outer shell), snail (soft-bodied – lives in a 'house' or shell), worms (have segments), fish (live in water, they have gills), amphibians (frog – starts life in water, ends up on land as well), reptiles (have scaly bodies – e.g. crocodiles, alligators), birds (warm-blooded, with feathers), mammals (warm-blooded, with hair).

Your child can find examples to fit into each group either from reference books or from the garden. A hand-lens or microscope is useful for examining insects. She can make up a little book with the group name written on each page.

insects		*snail group*	
fly	ant	slugs	mussels
bee	beetle	snails	whelks
wasp	caterpillar	cockles	winkles

crab group	*worms*		
crabs	earthworm		
lobsters	lugworm		
	ragworm		

fish	*amphibians*	*reptiles*	*birds*
shark	frog	crocodile	ostrich
freshwater fish	toad	alligator	eagles
sea-fish		newt	
cod, haddock etc.		snakes	
goldfish		lizards	

mammals

apes and monkeys		whales	cats
elephants	dogs		

Meteorological Symbols

These will begin to help your child understand weather charts.

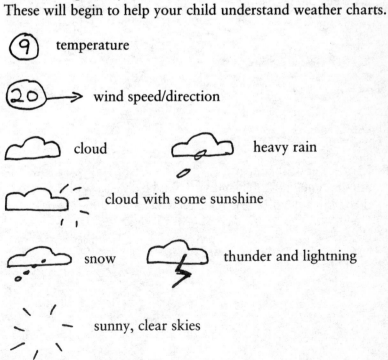

temperature

wind speed/direction

cloud   heavy rain

cloud with some sunshine

snow   thunder and lightning

sunny, clear skies

References (Weather)

Ash, Max and Charlotte, *Disastrous Hurricanes and Tornadoes*, Franklin Watts 1981

Green, Chris, and Rod, James, *Investigating Weather*, Arnold Wheaton 1985

Vibrations in air and materials

You can illustrate vibrations to your child through a number of simple exercises:

- Put a fork handle between the teeth, depress the prongs gently and let go allowing your child to feel the vibrations.
- She can also press down a ruler at the corner of a table and let go to feel the vibrations.
- Vibrations from a plucked guitar string can be heard.
- The association between music and vibration can be explored further by blowing across the top of an empty milk bottle. Then by filling it part-way with water it will produce a higher pitched sound.

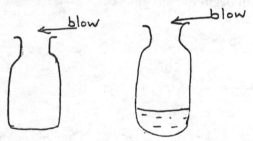

- Cut the end of a straw to the shape shown, press the triangular ends together and you will be able to produce music through the 'pipes'. The shorter straws have higher notes.

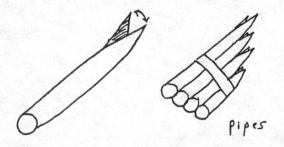

- A line of marbles will illustrate to your child how vibrations travel through materials:

- Vibrations can be seen if a tuning fork is set vibrating and put in water. The sound of the tuning fork can also be heard through wood and other materials.
- Stretch some string or twine tight between two yoghurt cups and make a 'telephone'. The vibrations of speech will pass through to the other yoghurt cup.

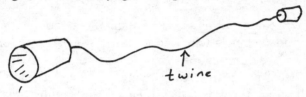

Force

Here are some ways to demonstrate how energy is produced:

- Get your child to spin an egg, then stop it. When she takes her hand off the egg it will continue spinning because of the energy that has been produced. Point out that the contents will go on spinning when the shell has stopped.
- Play with a yo-yo. It shows a similar 'stored' force when it climbs up the string.
- Release a stretched rubber band.

Forces in everyday life

Explain to your child examples of force that can easily be seen and felt. Here are some suggestions:

lifting

football

snooker

golf

car brakes

An electrical circuit

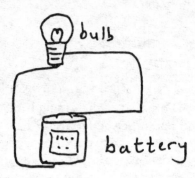

Set up a circuit by using some plasticine to stand a battery on a surface and sticking a wire to one side of the battery. Your child can then place different materials between the loose wire and the other side of the battery to see which allow electricity to flow through them. Try wood, metal, pencil lead, rubber, plastic.

The seasons and living things

As in the previous chapter describe the seasons and also the effect they have on living things. Here are some examples:

The migration of birds Some birds come to Britain in the summer and leave again before the onset of winter. Others arrive during the winter. Help your child to find out about migration from reference books.

Hibernation Certain animals such as bears, dormice and tortoises sleep through the winter.

Trees Some trees lose their leaves in winter. Point out the different trees and bushes that do this.

Sustaining Life

There is much to explain and talk about here. Here are some topics for discussion: Most plants make food. Animals consume it. Animals breathe, feed, move, multiply and react to the environment. This will mean most to your child when he considers his own environment and what he and other animals he has contact with do. Remind your child that he too needs food, water, air and that he moves, that he has reactions (e.g. hot things hurt), and adults have children.

GRADED TESTS
FOR 7 TO 9 YEAR OLDS

ENGLISH

TEST 1

(1)   Use these words to describe the pictures below:
heavy/light   day/night   sad/happy   young/old
right/wrong   out/in

....

....

....

....

(2)   Fit these words to the right pictures:
      castle, firework, church, caught, laugh, mountain, aeroplane

....

....

TEST 2

What am I?
(1)   I teach children ....
(2)   I sell food in a shop ....
(3)   I treat people who are ill ....
(4)   I sell medicines ....
(5)   I look after people's teeth ....
(6)   I fly an aeroplane ....

What makes these sounds?
 (7)   bark ....
 (8)   purr ....
 (9)   croak ....
(10)   roar ....
(11)   quack ....
(12)   hoot ....

What makes these sounds?

(13) tick ....

(14) drip ....

(15) bang ....

(16) slam ....

TEST 3

Name these groups:

(1) lion, dog, elephant ....

(2) coat, trousers, hat ....

(3) ant, fly, bee ....

(4) rose, daffodil, daisy ....

(5) bread, butter, sugar, cornflakes ....

Mark the 'odd' one out:

(6) eye, nose, mouth, hand, ear, collar, finger

(7) apple, orange, banana, oak, potato, plum

(8) carrot, potato, onion, lemonade

(9) whale, car, house, ship, pin

(10) boots, shoes, hat, slippers, curtains

Arrange in order of size, from smallest to biggest:

(11) ten, hundred, thousand, seventy-five

(12) hour, year, second, week, minute

(13) cm, km, m, mm

(14) kettle, cup, teapot, bucket, swimming pool

TEST 4

(1) Spider is to fly as cat is to ....

(2) North is to South as East is to ....

(3) Hand is to arm as foot is to ....

(4) Cat is to kitten as dog is to ....

(5) Walk is to legs as fly is to ....

(6) Bird is to air as fish is to ....

Complete each sentence with the right word:

(7)   I went to see my .... (ant, aunt).

(8)   He went to .... a toy (buy, by).

(9)   The .... ran through the forest
(dear, deer).

(10) The paper .... away (blue, blew).

(11) I had .... for dinner (meat, meet).

(12) .... house is over ....
(there, their).

(13) 'Don't .... at me!' (stair, stare).

(14) The .... in the sky is hot (son, sun).

TEST 5

Correct these sentences:

(1)   John has broke his leg.

(2)   There is six books on the chair.

(3)   Me and my friend went home.

(4)   It was me what did it.

(5)   Put capital letters and full stops in the following:

my class went to the london zoo today i had two pound to
spend i had a ride on a camel called sara later i bought an ice
cream i put it on a seat for one second and my teacher mrs
hutchins sat on it she got very cross and i got the blame i
don't know why because she was the one who sat on the ice
cream

Complete each sentence with the right word.

(6)   I made a cake with .... (flour, flower).

(7)   I can .... well over ....
(hear, here).

(8)   I ate a .... orange (hole, whole).

(9)   I left .... house an .... early
(our, hour).

(10) I bought a .... pencil (knew, new).

TEST 6

Unjumble these sentences:

(1)   Shops can go to now I the?

(2)   Much how doggy window the is in that?

(3)   Fireworks on night cat hid my cupboard in the.

(4)   football hate love but I I because many too Maths sums there are

(5)   Correct the wrongly spelt words:

Mi naym is Benny. I liv wiv mi mum and dad in a hows at the seesyde. It is veree borin heer in the winter becos nobodee cums. In the summr lots of peepol cum and lie on the beech getin sunbern. When they ar fed up wiv sunbern an crabs thay orl go home and liv happly ever after. Wye thay cum heer I don't no.

(**Note to parent:** this passage is most suitable for 9-year-olds, or good spellers.)

What are the words for these?

(6)   A man who works on a ship. ....

(7)   Where a car is put. ....

(8)   A hundred years. ....

(9)   The first meal of the day. ....

(10)   The instrument that measures heat (and cold)....................

TEST 7

(1)   Read the passage and answer the questions below.

Peter and the Polti

It seemed just like any other day when Peter came downstairs to eat his breakfast. Mum was in the kitchen busy burning the toast, Peter's big sister, Mary, was rushing around screaming, 'Where are my clean socks?'

The dog was in his usual place, hiding under the table with his paws stuck in his ears, and dear old Grandma was sitting in the only comfy armchair, busy knitting a purple jumper for Uncle Bert in Australia (Peter noted that it was now just about the right size for some huge gorilla to slip on).

Peter sat down for breakfast and tried to ignore the fuss going on around him but it was no use. 'Get out of my way!'

shrieked his sister, pushing him aside to grab the last piece of burnt toast. Peter suddenly felt depressed. Today was turning out to be worse than usual. Perhaps he was going to starve to death as well as having to go to school.

Suddenly, the tomato sauce bottle on the table in front of him began to move. Slowly, it rose into the air, unscrewed its own top and moved across until it was directly above the horrible Mary. Then it turned itself upside down and discharged tomato sauce all over her silky, blond hair. 'Arrh!' she gasped as the red ooze slipped down her face and on to her clean school blouse.

Peter watched as the tomato sauce bottle screwed its own top back on and set itself back on the table again. Now, this was more interesting! Perhaps today was going to be a better day, after all.

By Ken Adams

Questions

(a)   Why was the dog hiding under the table?

(b)   Where was Grandma sitting?

(c)   Why did Peter think about a gorilla?

(d)   What made Peter think that today was going to be a better day?

(e)   What do you think made the tomato sauce bottle rise into the air?

Put the correct words into these sentences:

(2)   He had a .... of shoes (pair, pear).

(3)   It was .... hot .... go .... the seaside for .... days (too, to, two).

TEST 8

(1)   Read the passage and answer the questions below.

Kiki the Parrot

They shut the trap-door quietly and then, in the pitch darkness, hid behind the stone archway near the door. They heard Joe putting a key into the lock. The door swung open, and the man appeared, looking huge in the flickering light of his lantern. He left the door open and went towards the back of the cellar, where the stores lay.

The boys had on rubber shoes and could have slipped out without Joe knowing anything at all – but Kiki chose that moment to imitate Joe's hollow cough. It filled the cellar with mournful echoes, and Joe dropped his lantern with a crash. The glass splintered and the light went out. Joe gave a howl of terror and fled out of the door at once, not even pausing to lock it. He brushed against the two boys as he went, and gave another screech of fright, feeling their warm bodies as he passed.

Kiki, thrilled at the result of her coughing imitation, gave an unearthly screech that sent Joe headlong through the other part of the cellar, up the steps and through the cellar door. He almost fell as he appeared in the kitchen, and Aunt Polly jumped in astonishment.

'What's the matter? What has happened?'

'There's things down there!' panted Joe, his face looking as scared as it ever could look.

From *Castle of Adventure* by Enid Blyton

Questions

(a) What was special about the boys wearing rubber shoes?

(b) Why did Joe drop his lantern with a crash?

(c) In the dark Joe brushed against the two boys. Why did he give a further screech of fright?

(d) What did Joe mean when he said, 'There's things down there'?

(e) Why was Kiki the parrot 'thrilled at the result of her coughing imitation'?

(f) What did Kiki do as a result?

(2) Write a letter to your aunt thanking her for your birthday present.

(3) Correct the spelling in this letter:

Deer Arnt Sal,

Fank yu for mi present wot yu sent me. Mi mum sed I must rite to yu becus it is polyte. Only, I didn lyke yore present. Yu ar nice but yore present is useless. Didn yu no I am grown up now an don't wont a Teddy Bare wiv a pink ribon. Enyway, I gayv it to mi sistr and she didn wont it eyether. She gayve it to owr dog, hoo has riped it into litel peeces. So fanks for yore bare present.

Luv, Benny.

(4)   Complete the crossword puzzle:

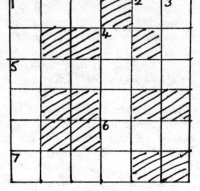

ACROSS
(1)   opposite of 'night'
(2)   opposite of 'down'
(5)   the cat .... the mouse
(6)   Pen and ....
(7)   ...., ... go
        away, come again
        another day

DOWN
(1)   He makes us better
(3)   To tap gently
(4)   To do it over

MATHEMATICS

TEST 1

(1)   24
       +   12
       ‾‾‾‾‾‾‾

(2)   36
       −   24
       ‾‾‾‾‾‾‾

(3)   What number does the 5 stand for in 542? ....
(4) $6 \times 2 =$ ....
(5) $2 \times 5 =$ ....
(6) $2 \times 10 =$ ....
(7) $5 \times 10 =$ ....
(8)   What are the times on these clocks?

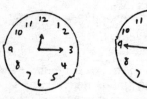

....

(9)   24
       +   16
       ‾‾‾‾‾‾‾

(10)   37
       −   21
       ‾‾‾‾‾‾‾

TEST 2

(1) × 5
          2
     _____

(2) × 10
          3
     _____

(3) × 5
          6
     _____

(4) + 77
          25
     _____

(5) − 36
          17
     _____

(6) − 40
          25
     _____

(7) + 75
          18
     _____

(8) + 84
          58
     _____

(9) − 56
          29
     _____

(10) How many pence?

(a) 50p 10p 5p 2p 1p 1p = ...
(b) 50p 2p 2p 2p 5p 10p = ...

(11) I buy a book which costs 36p with
      a 50p piece. How much change do I get? ....

(12)

The book costs 36p

(a) How much do *two* books cost? ....

(b) How much change do I get from £1
     if I buy one book? ....

TEST 3

(1) Write one pound ten pence in figures: ....

(2) × 21
          2
     _____

(3) × 34
          2
     _____

(4) How many pence in £1.24? ....

(5) A book costs £1.50 and a toy costs 80p.
     How much is that altogether? ....

(6) If one toy costs 65p, what do three toys cost? ....

(7) What are the times on these clocks?

....

(8) 2 ⟌ 8   (9) 2 ⟌ 12

☺ ☺☺☺   ☺ ☺☺☺☺ ☺

(10) 2 ⟌ 10

☺ ☺☺ ☺ ☺

(**Note to parent:** these sums are best done with buttons
or marbles at first.)

TEST 4

(1) How many centimetres are there in 1 metre?

     ....

(2) How many centimetres in ½ metre?

(3) 1 cm = ... mm

(4) ½ cm = ... mm

(5) 2 ⟌ 16   (7) 5 ⟌ 30

(6) 5 ⟌ 10   (8) 10 ⟌ 30

(9)   What are the times on these clocks?

....

(10)   What fraction are the shaded portions?

....

(11)   If I add 3 to a number I get 7.
        What is the number? ....

(12)   1 kilogram = ... g

(13)   ½ kilogram = ... g

TEST 5

(1)   324   (2)   452
       + 138   − 135
       _____   _____

(3)   225   (4)   32
       ×   2   ×   5
       _____   _____

(5) 2 ⟌ 5 remainder .... (6) 2 ⟌ 11 remainder ....

(7) 2 ⟌ 30   (8) 2 ⟌ 34

(9) ¼ kilogram = ... g

(10)

  (a) Which is bigger, $\frac{1}{2}$ or $\frac{1}{4}$?

  (b) $\frac{1}{2} = \frac{}{4}$

  (c) $\frac{1}{4} + \frac{1}{4} = \frac{}{4} = \frac{}{2}$

  (d) $\frac{3}{4} - \frac{1}{4} = \frac{}{4}$

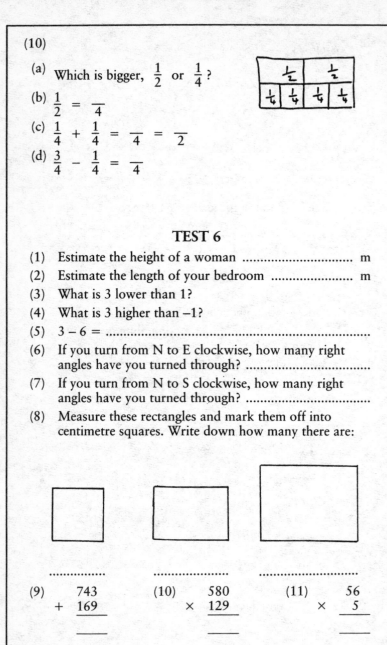

TEST 6

(1) Estimate the height of a woman .... m

(2) Estimate the length of your bedroom .... m

(3) What is 3 lower than 1?

(4) What is 3 higher than −1?

(5) $3 - 6 = $ ....

(6) If you turn from N to E clockwise, how many right angles have you turned through? ....

(7) If you turn from N to S clockwise, how many right angles have you turned through? ....

(8) Measure these rectangles and mark them off into centimetre squares. Write down how many there are:

       ....

(9)   743   (10)   580   (11)   56
    + 169   × 129   × 5

(12) $5 \overline{)\ 80}$

(13) What is the next number? 1, 2, 4, 7, ...

(14)   Complete the other halves of these letters

— Ⴀ—   — ⌒—   .D.   -⊔-

(15)   How many quarters in two whole ones? ....

(16)   How many 2p pieces in 20p? ....

(17)   How many quarters in $1\frac{1}{2}$? ....

(18)   How many pence in £0.12? ....

(19)   How many 10p pieces in £1.70? ....

CHAPTER SIX

YOUR CHILD
FROM NINE
TO ELEVEN

By these ages, patterns of thinking have often been established. Many a 10- or 11-year-old says, 'I'm no good at Maths' or 'I am hopeless at English', and behaves accordingly. Obviously, there are many reasons for not doing well in a certain subject and every case has to be looked at from an individual standpoint. However, every child can be helped by increased knowledge and understanding of the basic elements of Maths and English.

At no stage in this book has an attempt been made to assess so-called 'intelligence'. Clearly, some children are quicker at assimilating knowledge and are better at retaining it, and often the same children are quicker at grasping a concept. Even so-called 'intelligence', though, may be affected by such factors as lack of confidence and an adult's perception of a certain child, lack of knowledge of both syllabus elements and understanding of prerequisite concepts, and also by other motivational factors which are affected by the emotions.

One of the major difficulties that I have encountered over the years is the effect that labelling a child at 5 or 6 has on the attainment of that child by the time he reaches 10 or 11. The infant child's ability, or lack of ability, to conform to the class-room situation markedly affects its progress through school. It may be that teachers perceive children who have deficiencies in certain areas as being less bright overall. Jeffrey has always had difficulty with drawing. He writes badly and when he talks he gives the impression that he is much slower than a normal child. He has been classified as remedial for years and has little confidence in his abilities. Yet, with help at home, he has just succeeded in obtaining C grades in 7 G.C.S.E.s. (His school said that he would get rock bottom grades in all his subjects.) His only real difficulty is that he has come to accept failure as part of his life. Now, of course, with exam success he can start to rebuild his life.

Adults and children

A similar situation applies to many children coming to the end of their time at primary school. It is convenient for the school to categorise them. It would, of course, be immensely time-consuming for the school to investigate the real reasons for failure. I remember reading about one fourth-year junior boy who was labelled by his head teacher as not worthy of special Maths tuition for the Grammar School Entrance Exam. In spite of this he passed and in the Secondary School showed such a flair for Maths that his teacher put him in for A level when he was 12. He passed and became something of a 'celebrity'.

It is unfortunate if a child has a personality clash with a teacher. Robert was in this group and his work suffered badly for a year. Now, he has blossomed and is happy again with a new teacher and he has rapidly moved from the middle of the class to the top as his extra homework takes effect. He is more intelligent now, not only because he appears so, but because his scores in reasoning tests have markedly improved.

A parent can also inhibit their child's progress by increasing anxiety to such a level that it impedes learning. Over motivation by a parent can cause such anxiety that inhibitory processes are set in train. The remedy is to spend some time convincing the child and parent, that the work is not *that* important.

Some parents are notoriously impatient with their child. They 'jump' in to force an answer from him when he does not reply immediately. Some of these parents are teachers themselves who would never dream of being so oppressive with a child in their own class. If one attribute is essential in a good teacher it is *patience.* We must try and try again, to raise that glimmer of understanding in a child. A child's ability to succeed will inevitably suffer unless his teacher is patient because in the resultant anxious state of mind the child cannot begin to think – the infamous exam scenario where the mind goes 'blank'. Some anxiety, however, is necessary for motivation. Lethargy can result in a considerable dampening of the thought processes while over-anxiety can stop the whole process completely.

Examples of some 10- and 11-year-olds

Sadia suffers from panic when faced with Maths problems, but if she has been put at ease by a humorous remark, her ability seems to improve considerably. Claire is similar. In creative writing, however, none of this anxiety exists and both these girls have good, original ideas.

Many children of these ages do not read enough. Television, to a large extent, has taken the place of recreational reading. Reading, of course, demands a certain amount of mental effort while watching television requires very little. Boys seem to read much less than girls, and girls, in general, are better at creative writing at this age. This is particularly true of children from the ethnic minorities, especially Asians, where it is accepted that boys are good at Maths and girls are good at English.

Increased reading always results in an improvement in English. Parents do realise this and they take their child to the library and buy books, but often they say, 'he never reads it'. Comprehension exercises can help. These involve a considerable amount of reading and thinking about the narrative but they cannot ever replace the joy of reading a good story. Roald Dahl, Enid Blyton and certain authors like Judy Blume (*Superfudge*) are still able to lure children away from the television.

Children of this age have many gaps in their understanding, particularly in Maths, and this naturally hinders progress. Sandra had difficulty with fractions because she could not cancel and she had difficulty with cancelling because she did not understand division properly. Furthermore, she was never taught her tables. Her schooling coincided with the era when the learning of tables was considered 'wicked' because they were imposed, rote-learnt. Her division is so laboured that she loses concentration and gives up easily.

Pupils in one school I know are under-achieving considerably because the school believes in learning by discovery and does not provide clear objectives. The children are floundering around trying to discover what it is they are supposed to discover. However, one boy from this school does extra work at home and soaks up everything given to him and he is thrilled with his success. While his schoolmates learn little but frustration, he moves on, leaving them far behind.

Catherine is quick thinking but over the years has adapted badly to the classroom situation. She once needed individual help and encouragement but did not get it. Now, at 11, she has adopted an attitude more common among 14- and 15-year-olds: 'I couldn't care less.' It masks a deep need to succeed, to please her mother who wants her to do better than she did. However, there are real problems because work has been associated over a long period with bad results. She has been subjected to persistent aversion therapy. She needs constant encouragement and more rewards for effort than most children.

Jonathan long ago convinced himself that he was not clever. It is difficult to persuade him from putting aside a problem after a cursory glance and announcing, 'that is too hard for me'. Usually, it is not. After persuasion he tries the problem and, with a struggle, does it.

Finally, even those who have had home tuition, for many years continue to have problems. They know and understand all the major elements of Maths and English and have developed appropriate schemas to deal with most problems, but they are over-confident. They are often impatient with a new problem that arises and dismiss it too quickly, not allowing time for the various elements of the problem to link with already developed schemas in their long-term memory. 'Slow down,' I say, 'allow your mind time to digest the information.'

Among the well-taught in this age group, the differences in performance often reflect *real* differences in flair and ability, because problems of confidence, lack of understanding and knowledge have already been eliminated. A clearer picture of a child's real potential begins to emerge at this stage, although this may still not be fully realised if his progress is not monitored through his time spent at Secondary School. Failure is always a short step away.

ENGLISH

Spelling

These words are grouped according to similar letter strings.

cure   sure   fury   jury   plural

your   court   pour   favour   harbour

picture   capture   fracture   mixture   temperature

try   cry   marry   empty   worry

tried   cried   married   emptied   worried

love   like   eat   laugh

lovable   likeable   eatable   laughable

possible   horrible   terrible   sensible   visible

comical   usual   equal   medal   royal

camel   tunnel   label   towel   model

careful   helpful   cupful   awful   beautiful

battle   little   apple   middle   cycle

bang   bung   song   long   wrong

comic   picnic   traffic   Atlantic   Arctic

bondage   cabbage   savage

bridge   hedge   ridge   ledge   budge

million   region   onion   religion

division   television   passion

kindness   goodness   happiness

bought   fought   thought

caught   taught   naughty   daughter

trough   rough   cough   tough   enough   bough   though
through

disturbance   entrance

science   difference   commence

rogue   plague   league   fatigue

biology   geology   zoology

musician   politician   magician   electrician   physician

Homophones

These are words sounding alike but with different meanings.

allowed	aloud		made	maid	
ball	bawl		mare	mayor	
beach	beech		meat	meet	
bean	been		medal	meddle	
beat	beet		missed	mist	
blew	blue		none	nun	
boy	buoy		pail	pale	
brake	break		peal	peel	
buy	by		pair	pear	
cell	sell		pause	paws	
cereal	serial		peace	piece	
cent	sent	scent	peer	pier	
coarse	course		plain	plane	
currant	current		rain	reign	
dear	deer		raise	rays	
fair	fare		rap	wrap	
feat	feet		read	reed	
find	fined		right	write	
flour	flower		ring	wring	
groan	grown		road	rowed	rode
hair	hare		sail	sale	
heel	heal		scene	seen	
hear	here		son	sun	
heard	herd		stair	stare	
him	hymn		steal	steel	
hole	whole		tail	tale	
hour	our		their	there	
knew	new		tide	tied	
knight	night		vain	vein	
knot	not		waist	waste	
knows	nose		weak	week	
lead	led		wood	would	

Reading

Much of your child's writing comes from a conscious or uncon-
scious imitation of what he reads in books. Samina, for instance,
writes 10,000-word stories, usually thinly disguised imitations
of American school life sagas. Her stories are original and have
conflict although that is invariably of the slanging match variety,
rather like a television soap. In order to improve she needs to
develop a steady, rising conflict within a strong story framework
and to try to think of a 'twist' to the tale.

Books The following is a reading list suitable for this age group.
Many of these titles are also available in paperback editions.

Adams, Richard, *Watership Down*, Allen Lane 1982

Aiken, Joan, *Anabel's Raven*, BBC 1990

Bawden, Nina, *Carrie's War*, Gollancz 1973

Blume, Judy, *Tales of a Fourth Grade Nothing*, The Bodley
   Head 1979

Boston, Lucy M., *The Children of Green Knowe*, Faber 1954

Burnett, Frances Hodgson, *The Secret Garden*, Gollancz 1989
   (many other editions)

Carroll, Lewis, *Alice in Wonderland*, many editions

Cross, Gillian, *The Demon Headmaster*, Oxford University
   Press 1982

Dahl, Roald, *Charlie and the Chocolate Factory*, Allen and Unwin
   1985; *Charlie and the Great Glass Elevator*, Allen and Unwin
   1986

Dickens, Charles, *A Christmas Carol*, Blackie 1986 (many other
   editions); *The Old Curiosity Shop*, Collins 1973

Frank, Anne, *The Diary of Anne Frank*, Heinemann 1990

Garner, Alan, *The Owl Service*, Windrush 1987

Goscinny, René, and Uderzo, Albert, *Asterix the Gaul*, Hodder
   1969

Graham, Kenneth, *Wind in the Willows*, Methuen 1971 (many
   other editions)

'Herge', *Adventures of Tintin*, Vols. 1 & 2, Methuen 1989

Hinton, Nigel, *Beaver Towers*, Hodder 1983

Hunter, Norman, *Professor Branestawm* series, The Bodley Head and Penguin

Juster, Norton, *The Phantom Tollbooth*, Chivers Press 1989

Keene, Carolyne, The *Nancy Drew* Mysteries, Armada Books

Kemp, Gene, *The Turbulent Term of Tyke Tiler*, Collins 1984

King, Clive, *Stig of the Dump*, Viking Kestrel 1985

Lewis, C.S., *The Last Battle*, Collins 1989

Lively, Penelope, *The Ghost of Thomas Kempe*, Heinemann 1973

Montgomery, L.M., *Anne of Green Gables*, Harrap 1961

Norton, Mary, *The Borrowers*, Dent 1975

Ransome, Arthur, *Swallows and Amazons*, Cape 1930

Rosen, Michael, (illus, Blake, Quentin), *Quick Let's Get Out of Here*, Deutsch 1983; Ed., *Children's Poetry*, Kingfisher 1985

Sewell, Anna, *Black Beauty*, Michael O'Mara Books 1986 (many other editions)

Smith, Dodie, *One Hundred and One Dalmatians*, Grafton 1986

Tolkien, J.R.R., *The Hobbit*, Unwin Hyman 1987; *The Lord of the Rings*, Unwin Hyman 1988

Townsend, Sue, *The Adrian Mole Diaries: The Secret Diary of Adrian Mole, Aged Thirteen and Three Quarters*, Methuen 1985

Twain, Mark, *The Adventures of Huckleberry Finn*, Macmillan 1983

Wells, H.G., *The Time Machine*, Heinemann

Williamson, Henry, *Tarka the Otter*, Macmillan 1981

Wilson, Forrest, The *Super Gran* series, Penguin Books

Wyndham, John, *The Day of the Triffids*, Hutchinson 1975

Writing

In learning to write well, the aid of a dictionary and *Roget's Thesaurus* are invaluable. Your child should first write a piece freely and then be encouraged to re-write it taking care over punctuation, correcting spelling mistakes, re-structuring sentences and replacing over-repeated words or substituting better words. There are several other points to bear in mind, both when re-writing and when doing a first draft.

Scenes and incidents in a story should be varied and repetitions avoided. Steven aged 10, has just written about his involvement in a football tournament, but he simply wrote down a list of goals scored, by whom and in which round. Halfway through reading it I feel a great wave of boredom sweeping over me for I do not know the players and he is repeating similar goal-scoring incidents. Steven can improve his writing by mentioning results intermingled with descriptions of the venue, of colours, things people said, how he felt at the time, what the teacher did or said, and his own feelings before and after it was all over, and so on. He should, of course, read more and watch less television.

A story should essentially begin with an introduction to the characters involved; it should show conflict between those characters or between them and their environment; it should rise to a climax and then finish with a resolution. Incidents should link together within a story so that a beginning, middle and ending format is attained. A story should move, and this is helped by using active verbs rather than passive ones. For example, 'I ran up the stairs two at a time and slammed the door behind me' rather than 'I got dressed upstairs'.

Writing is improved immensely by a touch of humour and it should appeal to the senses wherever possible, particularly to sight, 'The garden was a blaze of colour – red, blue and golden-headed flowers nodded in the summer breeze' and sound, 'It was a noisy party full of chattering, shrieking children!' Other senses that could be involved are taste, touch and smell. For instance: 'When I came down to breakfast, I could smell the bacon sizzling in the frying pan.'

When using a *Thesaurus* it should be noted that many words of similar meaning are not always the ones a child would intend to use. For example, a child writing, 'the lady is nice' probably means 'the lady is kind' not 'the lady is beautiful'.

Some useful words and ideas for descriptive writing

People

Figure tall, short, lanky, stout, thin, fat, frail, athletic, bent, manly, powerful, gigantic, deformed, dwarf-like, delicate

Head and face round, oval, long, small, thin, fat, flat, wrinkled

Nose long, fat, snub, straight, broad, dainty, enormous

Hair straight, wavy, curly, coarse, fine, tangled, brown, grey, blonde, silvery, ginger, auburn, black, golden, long, silky, bobbed, plaited

Eyes clear, bright, large, small, brown, blue, green, grey, shy, beady, shifty, twinkling, sparkling

Skin tanned, pale, swarthy, fair, bronzed, sunburnt, ruddy, rough, smooth, freckled

Mouth, lips, teeth wide, thin, rose-bud, twisted, stained, bad, decayed, irregular, projecting, uneven

Character kind, proud, vain, greedy, selfish, miserable, affectionate, honest, humble, charming, spiteful, mean, loyal, generous, sincere, lovable, stubborn, obstinate, enthusiastic, timid, excitable, bold, impetuous

Clothing shirt, collar, tie, trousers, shorts, pants, bathing suit, shoes, socks, pyjamas, jumper, sweater, suit, jacket, overcoat, vest, blouse, dress, skirt, high heels, boots, stockings, tights, hat, cap, scarf, cuffs, gloves

Habits and characteristics drumming fingers, spitting, sniffing, coughing, putting one's head on one side, peering, quizzical, worried, troubled, smirking, laughing, giggling, sneering, limping, finger sucking, blinking, twitching, tapping a foot, upright, smart, ragged, untidy, dowdy, stroking chin/beard, brushing back hair, pulling an ear

Voice low, high-pitched, squeaky, shrill, hoarse, deep, harsh, grating, rasping, tenor, bass, pleasant, husky, nasal, quavering

Movement quick, slow, laboured, walking, running, leaping, clapping, writing, drawing, painting, washing, dusting, stroking, smacking, hitting, hanging, sawing, chopping

Sounds

Birds singing, chirping, whistling, hooting, fluttering, chattering, cawing

People shouting, crying, weeping, laughing, screaming, chatter-

ing, shrieking, tutting, giggling, groaning, moaning, muttering, whistling, singing, hum of voices
Nature leaves rustling, thunder clapping, rain beating and pattering, wind rushing, stream rushing, steam hissing, brook bubbling, water dripping/dribbling/gushing/rushing, mice squeaking, bees humming/buzzing, dogs barking, cats mewing, cows lowing, sheep bleating, horses neighing, lions roaring, elephants trumpeting
Things radio/television blaring out, tap dripping, crackling of a fire, things frying, bubbling of boiling water, clock ticking, door creaking

Smells flowers, roses, sweet peas, the farmyard, salt breeze, hot chestnuts, burnt toast, hot cakes, turkey in the oven, scent/perfume, old socks, onions, apples, bananas, strawberries, petrol, fish and chips

Taste sugar, salt, sweet, sour, bitter, acid, orange, fishy, fruity, meaty, tasty

Touch caress, gentle, stroke, fondle, smack, kiss, hug, squeeze, rub, punch, stab, pound, prod, poke

Colours green grass, green trees, red roses, yellow daffodils, blue sky, green/blue sea, yellow sand, rainbow, coloured flags, coloured dresses, ties and shirts, whitewashed walls, silver moon, golden sun, white clouds, coloured lights, hair colours, shoe colours, skin colours

Country scenes trees, fields, river, brook, geese, ducks, sparrows, cows, sheep, horses, farmyard, bull, goat, hills, marshes, oak, sycamore, holly, horse-chestnut, cones, fallen leaves, trout, pike, fishermen, church, thatched cottage, fête

Town scenes road, streets, traffic lights, shops, pavement, lamp-post, kerb, shop-window, town hall, market, stalls, supermarket, station, platform, train, library, café, buses, lorries, vans, taxis, policemen, umbrellas, department store, offices

Seaside sand, shore, waves, pier, fair, roundabouts, Big Wheel, rocks, cliffs, caves, fish, yachts, rowing boats, liners, hotel, boarding house, pebbles, sea breeze, deck chairs

A room shape, decoration, windows, ceiling, floor-covering, heating, lighting, furniture

Joined up writing

By the age of 9, your child will need to start joining up letters so that he will attain a fast flowing hand by the time he leaves primary school. The following is a useful guide.

Letters joined diagonally

acdehiklmntu

Sharp joins

iuy

Rounded joins

nmr

Horizontal joins

forvw

Letters with no 'after' join

b g j p q s x y z

Capitals These stand entirely separate.

The quick brown fox jumps over the lazy dog.

Punctuation

Speech Marks By the age of 9 or 10 your child should be skilled in the use of speech marks (' '). A common error, however, is to embrace not only written speech, but also the speaker with them:

'Come on home said John'

Another error is to put exclamation and question marks *outside* the marks:

'What is your name'?

Children also miss commas and capitals:

'hello'   said the girl.

Question marks and exclamation marks These are very effective in qualifying what a child is trying to say. Roald Dahl, for example, uses the exclamation mark to great effect. 'How can that be?' asked the man. 'Be quiet!' shouted the teacher.

Commas The most important ones occur in lists:

'Racing along the highway were cars, lorries, buses and motor-cycles.'

MATHEMATICS

Shopping sums
By now these should be formalised. Insist that your child writes down every sum in a clear manner:

Cost £	Change £
0.36	5.00
+ 1.43	− 1.79
1.79	3.21

Extension of tables

$1 \times 3 =$ ○ ○ ○ $= 3$ $1 \times 4 =$ ○ ○ ○ ○ $= 4$

$2 \times 3 = 6$ $2 \times 4 = 8$

$3 \times 3 = 9$ $3 \times 4 = 12$

$4 \times 3 = 12$ $4 \times 4 = 16$

$5 \times 3 = 15$ $5 \times 4 = 20$

$6 \times 3 = 18$ $6 \times 4 = 24$

$7 \times 3 = 21$ $7 \times 4 = 28$

$8 \times 3 = 24$ $8 \times 4 = 32$

$9 \times 3 = 27$ $9 \times 4 = 36$

$10 \times 3 = 30$ $10 \times 4 = 40$

$1 \times 6 =$ ○ ○ ○ ○ ○ ○ $= 6$ $1 \times 7 =$ ○ ○ ○ ○ ○ ○ ○ $= 7$

$2 \times 6 = 12$ $2 \times 7 = 14$

$3 \times 6 = 18$ $3 \times 7 = 21$

$4 \times 6 = 24$ $4 \times 7 = 28$

$5 \times 6 = 30$ $5 \times 7 = 35$

$6 \times 6 = 36$ $6 \times 7 = 42$

$7 \times 6 = 42$ $7 \times 7 = 49$

$8 \times 6 = 48$ $8 \times 7 = 56$

$9 \times 6 = 54$ $9 \times 7 = 63$

$10 \times 6 = 60$ $10 \times 7 = 70$

$1 \times 8 = \circ\circ\circ\circ\circ\circ\circ\circ = 8$ $1 \times 9 = \circ\circ\circ\circ\circ\circ\circ\circ\circ = 9$

$2 \times 8 = 16$ $2 \times 9 = 18$

$3 \times 8 = 24$ $3 \times 9 = 27$

$4 \times 8 = 32$ $4 \times 9 = 36$

$5 \times 8 = 40$ $5 \times 9 = 45$

$6 \times 8 = 48$ $6 \times 9 = 54$

$7 \times 8 = 56$ $7 \times 9 = 63$

$8 \times 8 = 64$ $8 \times 9 = 72$

$9 \times 8 = 72$ $9 \times 9 = 81$

$10 \times 8 = 80$ $10 \times 9 = 90$

Often children will ask to be allowed to write out all the 'bubbles' and contents for a particular table.

Fractions

Equivalence Equivalence in value can be illustrated by cutting out strips of paper to represent fractions:

$$\frac{1}{2} = \frac{2}{4} = \frac{4}{8}$$

$\frac{1}{2}$		$\frac{1}{2}$	
$\frac{1}{4}$	$\frac{1}{4}$	$\frac{1}{4}$	$\frac{1}{4}$

$\frac{1}{8}$ $\frac{1}{8}$ $\frac{1}{8}$ $\frac{1}{8}$ $\frac{1}{8}$ $\frac{1}{8}$ $\frac{1}{8}$ $\frac{1}{8}$

$\frac{1}{2} + \frac{1}{2} = 1$

$\frac{1}{4} + \frac{1}{4} + \frac{1}{4} + \frac{1}{4} = 1$

$\frac{1}{8} + \frac{1}{8} + \frac{1}{8} + \frac{1}{8} + \frac{1}{8} + \frac{1}{8} + \frac{1}{8} + \frac{1}{8} = 1$

After a long period of consolidation and only then should a more formal presentation be used:

$$\frac{1 \times 2}{2 \times 2} = \frac{2}{4} \quad \text{or} \quad \frac{4 \div 4}{8 \div 4} = \frac{1}{2}$$

Even then, there is difficulty in a child visualising a connection between the purely operational multiplication/division and the equivalence concept. The establishment of links such as this is important if meaning is to be made of operations in Maths.

Further work on fractions

The idea of the division of one whole into a number of equivalent fractions escapes many children. Time needs to be spent establishing this concept, particularly the division of one whole into ten parts and one hundred parts, because this is vital in understanding decimals and percentages.

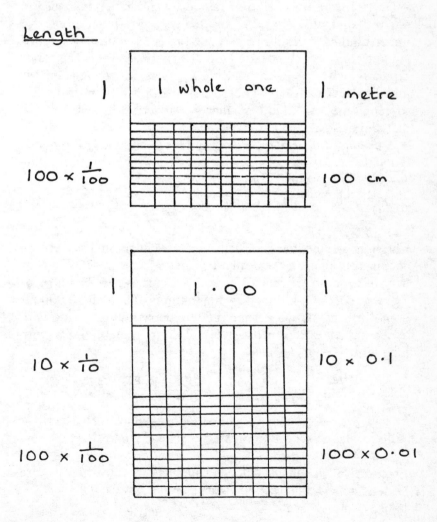

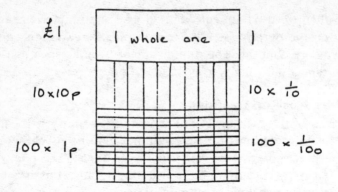

Decimals are not well understood by children. They need to see the equivalence of $^1/_{10}$ to 0.1 very clearly in order for understanding to result. Diagrammatic representation is important and considerable consolidation work is necessary. The major difficulty with decimals and the conversion of units is the inability to visualise links because of the difficulty in being able to represent 'big' numbers in real life either by pictures or diagrammatically.

A *distance line* is another way of representing length:

Children are, however, usually fairly clear about metres and centimetres because they often use metre sticks in school. They have much more difficulty visualising 1 cm^3 as part of a litre, or 1 mm as part of a kilometre – for example. 0.001 and 0.0001 is even further removed from their understanding. Work with 'place value' can sometimes establish meaningful links with long-term memory:

Fractions in Problems Once a child has established rules for understanding in fraction work, he is invariably 'lost' in problems with fractions such as: 'What is $\frac{1}{4}$ of 60?' This can be taught as follows:

(Step 1)

'What is $\frac{1}{4}$ of 8?' (substitute 8 for 60)
    Answer (immediately): '2'
'How did you do that?'
    Answer: 'I divided.' (Sometimes it is 'I timesed' –
    meaning 2 × 4 = 8.)
'What did you divide?'
    Answer: 'The 8 by the 4'
'Then, $\frac{1}{4}$ of 8 = 2. So what is $\frac{1}{4}$ of 60?'

(Leads to division) $\longrightarrow$

$$\begin{array}{r} 15 \\ 4\overline{)60} \end{array}$$

'What then is $\frac{3}{4}$ (emphasising *three*) of 60?'
    Answer: '15 + 15 + 15 = 45'

By breaking down problem-solving in this way links are provided between concepts and difficulties are overcome in visualising operations on 'bigger' numbers.

Reversing operations

$$6 \xrightarrow{+3} 9 \quad \text{and} \quad 4 \xrightarrow{\times 3} 12$$
$$6 \xleftarrow{-3} 9 \qquad\qquad 4 \xleftarrow{\div 3} 12$$

Reverse operations are illustrated by a problem like 'A father is four times as old as his son. The father is 48. How old is the son?'

$$? \xrightarrow{\times 4} 48$$
$$\boxed{12} \xleftarrow{\div 4}$$

The 24-hour clock and timetables

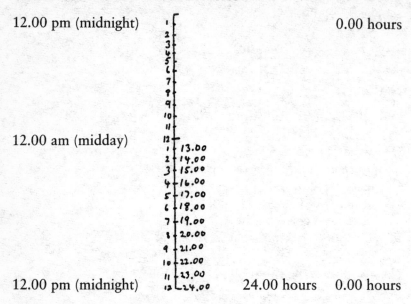

12.00 pm (midnight)   0.00 hours

12.00 am (midday)

12.00 pm (midnight)   24.00 hours   0.00 hours

A useful rule to learn here is that to change to 24-hour-clock times add 12 to all hours in p.m.

Timetables Local bus and train timetables are useful teaching aids. 'Visualising' the passing of time is extremely useful. An adult, for example, 'counts on' in hours and minutes between times. How else can one work out the length of time from 19.42 on Tuesday to 02.56 on Wednesday, without resorting to different sums? To grasp this idea your child will need to use a clock with movable hands every time he works out such a problem.

A child can best work out the passage of time by using a *line of time* as can be seen in this example.

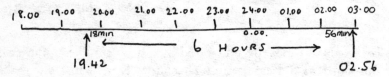

18 + 56 minutes = 1 hour 14 minutes

total time = 6 hours + 1 hour 14 minutes

= 7 hours 14 minutes

It is still necessary to teach the subtraction of time, however. The borrowing of 60 minutes (or seconds) is initially very confusing for a child:

hours	minutes		side sum

22 23 →60+ 34   8̷9̷'4
— 1 9   5 6   − 5 6
———————————————   ————
   3   3 8   3 8

The right units for the right things

Your child should have a clear idea that *millimetres* (mm) are for measuring the length of something small like a pin
centimetres (cm) are for most household objects
metres (m) are for paths, height of a house, heights of people, street lengths
kilometres (km) are used for distances between towns
grams (g) are used for the weight of small packets of sweets
kilograms (kg) are used for the weights of large packets of food, a man etc.
tonnes are used for whales and large lorries

Volume

Make a cube for your child from card using a net (or the shape of a 3-D figure when laid out flat) like the one below.

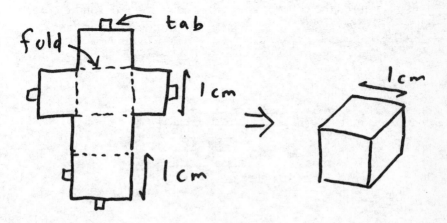

Tell your child that this is a one centimetre cube:

$$1cm \times 1cm \times 1cm$$

(length $\times$ width $\times$ height is 1cm^3)

If several of these are made up your child can appreciate the amount of space that these cubes take up. He can estimate how many centimetre cubes it will take to fill: a drawer, a cupboard, a box of cornflakes, a shoe, the sink, the bath, a room.

If you seal the cracks, he can see how much liquid will fill the cube. This provides a link with previous work on volume using liquids which have volume but no definite form.

Co-ordinates

Co-ordinates are used to fix the position of a point. A local map is a useful aid to teaching co-ordinates. A child can see the relevance to everyday life. Interest can be stimulated because he can find where *he* lives.

	1	2	3	4	
A			🏠		
B					
C				🚃	
D					
E					

I live at A,3

The station is at C,4

To reinforce the concept you will need centimetre square graph paper. Interest can be stimulated by joining points to make a shape (e.g. a boat, a train).

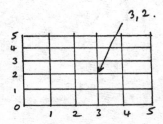

Nets

In addition to the above net of a cube, your child can make various shapes such as:

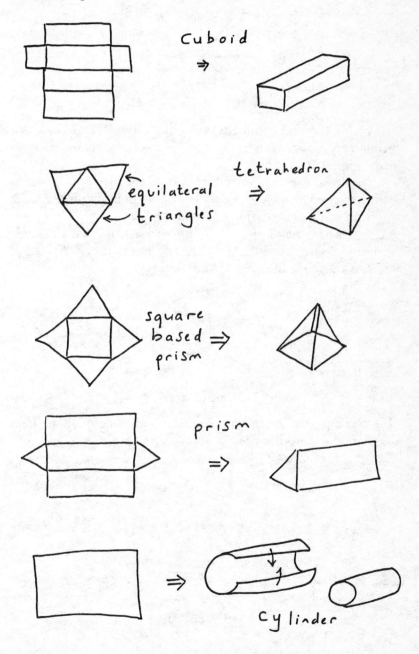

Cuboid ⇒

equilateral triangles

tetrahedron ⇒

square based prism ⇒

prism ⇒

⇒

Cylinder

Angles

The idea of angles can be extended by reference to the compass or clock:

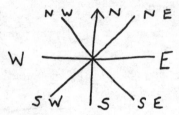

Tell your child, 'If I turn between N and NE or E and SE, I turn through 45°. Turning more than 90° is an *obtuse* angle, less is an *acute* angle.'

It would be useful to introduce him to the magnetic compass at this stage. The idea of a needle always pointing in the same direction can be fascinating to a child.

Using the big hand of a clock show your child that the angle between 12 and 1 is 30°. And then tell him that 3 × 30° is 90° which is the angle between 12 and 3.

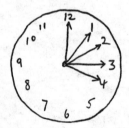

Using compasses A pair of compasses can be used to help illustrate the sizes of angles.

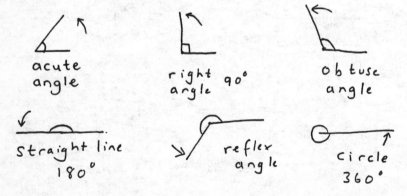

acute angle

right angle 90°

obtuse angle

straight line 180°

reflex angle

circle 360°

Perpendicular, horizontal and vertical On the compass line drawing, the N–S line is at right angles to the E–W line and *perpendicular* to it.

Horizontal and *vertical* can be taught by reference to objects around the house:

horizontal	*vertical*
floor	wall
ceiling	door
table top	chairlegs
pavement (not on a hill)	tree-trunk

vertical

horizontal

Rotation
Let your child rotate some tracing paper placed over an image through various angles to see where that image ends up.

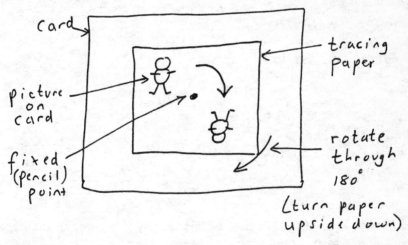

Card

tracing paper

picture on card

rotate through 180°

fixed (pencil) point

(turn paper upside down)

Average or mean
If a few like objects, e.g. sweets, are shared unequally between several people this concept can be demonstrated:

o o ooo o
6 sweets

o ooo
4 sweets

o o
2 sweets

'Unfair!' cries the child, who is then able to show a 'fair' sharing:

O O O O   O O O O   O O O O

Thus 4 is the *average* or *mean*.

Changing the number (of people and shared objects), and repeating the experience several times serves to illustrate the concept of *average*.

Chance or Probability

If your child is used to dice games, or throwing a coin for 'heads or tails', then he will already have an idea of chance.

At this age a child needs to know no more than *no chance*, *half chance* and *certainty*.

More than, less than

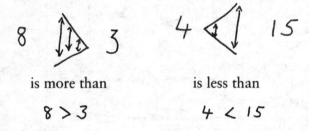

8   3   4   15

is more than   is less than

$8 > 3$ $4 < 15$

Always have a number line as an aid alongside sums so that he can see which is the bigger number:

$$2 > -6$$
$$(2 \text{ is bigger than } -6)$$

Useful calculators Calculators may be used by your child to check answers to their sums and investigate very small or very large numbers. (*See* also page 109.)

(1)   Casio
(2)   Sharp
(3)   Texas
(4)   Scientific calculators are useful for more advanced Primary work.

SCIENCE

In this section I mention various topics that you can work on with your child.

Fossils

You can find rocks that contain fossils of a variety of animals particularly among those that once lived under water. Sandstone, clay, shale, and limestone are good rocks to examine. Museums often contain rocks with imprints of small animals and plants.

A dinosaur is a relic. Dinosaurs dominated the earth for 135 million years. Then suddenly they died out and became extinct. Nobody knows how or why this disaster occurred. Skeletons of dinosaurs have been found in different parts of the world. Various museums contain bones or life-sized models of dinosaurs.

Triceratops

Parts of a plant

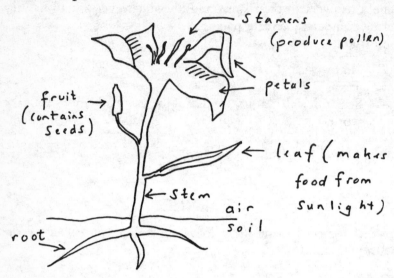

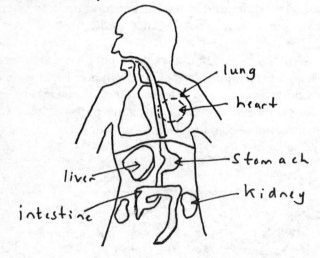

Organs of the body

Materials

Materials are substances we find in the world and that we use. Your child should be aware of the wide range of materials that exist. Air and water are the most common materials. There are also many new materials that are made from natural ones. As in the previous chapter ask your child to investigate the properties of: stone, brick, cement, pottery, metals, glass, paper, rubber, skins, hides, leather, hair, wool, plastics, diamond, graphite.

The three states of matter
Everything exists in the three states of matter either as solids, liquids or gases. Your child can add to the list by putting various *materials* in the different groups.

Solids	Liquids	Gases
ice	water	steam
iron	petrol	air
wood	alcohol	
plasticine	oil	
sugar	milk	

Your child can add to the list by putting various materials in the different groups.

Stone age tools A long time ago, men used stone to make axes, arrow heads and tools.

Metals
Iron and steel have many uses from making bridges to cutlery and pipes.
Aluminium is used in saucepans and aircraft.
Copper is used for wires. *Zinc and tin* protect iron from rusting.
Lead is a solder to join wires together. *Copper and brass* are used in ornaments.

Plastics
Plastic rubber nowadays replaces natural rubber from rubber trees.
PVC is used for shoes, boots, clothes, table cloths.
Polystyrene is used for packing.
Perspex is used in place of glass.

Graphite is used as a solid lubricant in cars and aeroplanes. Other materials in this category are: nylon, films, paints.

Weather

There is much to learn about the climate and weather. Here are a few ideas for discussion.

Instruments

A simple *plastic cup* can measure rainfall. If the top of the cup is 10 times bigger than the base, 10 cm in the cup measures 1 cm of rainfall.

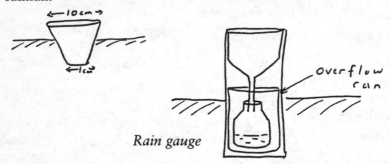

Rain gauge

Rainfall is collected in the gauge which is positioned off the ground and firmly fixed. The amount can be recorded on a graph with a block representing the level of rainfall each day. This is called a bar graph.

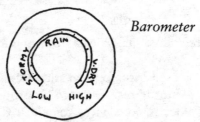

Barometer

A barometer records air pressure from different weights of air. Your child can record pressure changes and learn to relate them to the weather.

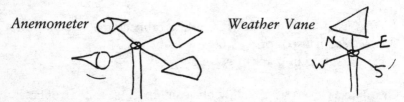

Anemometer   Weather Vane

This measures *wind speed.*   This measures wind *direction.*

The Beaufort Scale This denotes the force of the wind, measured and referred to in numbers up to Force 12 or hurricane force.

0. *calm*, smoke rises vertically

1. *light air*, smoke drifts

3. *gentle breeze*, clothes flap

2. *light breeze*, leaves rustle

4. *moderate breeze*, paper blows about

5. *fresh breeze*, crests on the waves

6. *strong breeze*, problems with umbrellas

7. *near gale*, whole trees bend in the wind

8. *gale*, small branches break off

9. *strong gale*, slates and bricks blown off

10. *whole gale*, trees uprooted

11. *storm*, cars blown off the road

12. *hurricane*

Weather hazards
Weather can mean life or death for some people. Hurricanes, tornadoes and whirlwinds can cause great devastation. Together with floods and hail they can destroy crops and civilisation. Frost in spring kills young plants. Drought (lack of water) kills plants and crops causing famine. The failure of the monsoon rains in India could start a drought and famine affecting millions.

A greenhouse

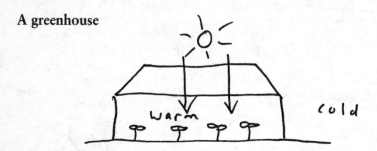

The heat from the sun is trapped within the glass of the greenhouse to produce a tropical atmosphere.

Greenhouse effect Carbon dioxide from burning coal, petrol, oil and wood acts like a greenhouse on the world, warming it up. This may have disastrous consequences environmentally.

Clouds and rain

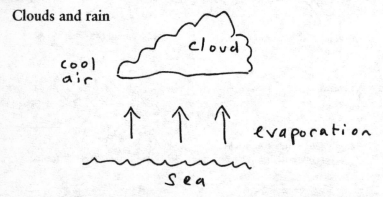

Water droplets rising from the sea join together to form larger drops in cooler air, thus forming cumulus clouds. There are two types of clouds – cumulus (heap) and stratus (layer). Layer clouds form when large areas of air are lifted.

Some clouds

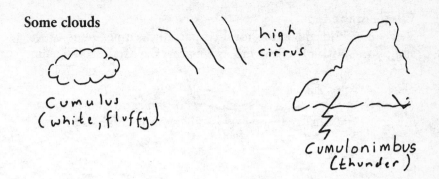

Fronts

Acid rain

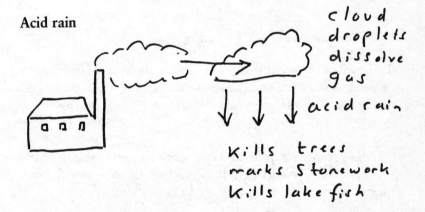

Acid rain is caused by rain drops dissolving acid gases from smoke emission.

The Solar System
Explain to your child about this – that the sun and its attendant planets and bodies move about it under *gravity*. The sun is a star like those we see at night.

Eclipse of the sun

Tell your child about the total or partial disappearance of the sun by the position of the moon between the earth and the sun.

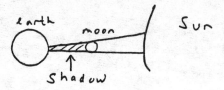

Eclipse of the moon

Similarly the eclipse of the moon occurs when the earth comes between it and the sun casting a shadow across it.

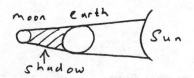

Light travels in straight lines How do we know this? Explain to your child that we know because we cannot see around corners. For instance, torch beams don't bend.

Forces

A force is a 'push' or 'pull' and can result in movement, stretching or squashing. Various kinds of forces act in our world. Here are some ideas to demonstrate this to your child.

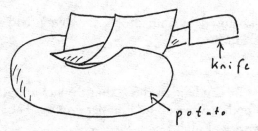

Try cutting a potato through a piece of paper. The paper stays uncut while the potato is cut because the particles of paper are closer together than those of the potato and so require more 'force'.

Weight is a force due to *gravity* when objects (and humans) are pulled downwards. It can be illustrated by the following examples:

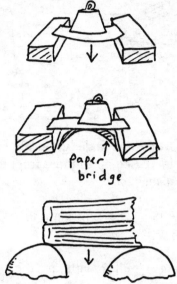

Round structures such as the paper bridge or egg shells above are strong in resisting the force of weight. Your child can investigate the effects of weight on different materials (e.g. plasticine). Introduce the idea of gravity pulling down on a weight and unbalancing things.

Balance

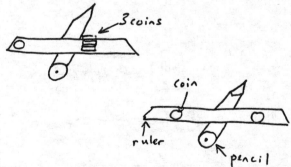

One coin balances another when they are equidistant from the pencil. Three coins balance one coin when one 'distance', as shown, is three times the other.

Overcoming forces
Investigate the number of coins needed to pull a single coin:

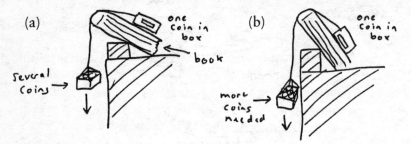

(a) one coin in box
book
several coins →
↓

(b) one coin in box
more coins needed →
↓

The box of coins moves down under gravity in (a) but when the angle of the book is increased in (b) more force is needed to pull the coin in the box at the top.

It needs little force to pull *up* a big weight in (b).

A pulley
Your child can make a pulley with the use of a few simple objects such as a cotton reel, wooden brick and some wire. He can attach it to a broom handle.

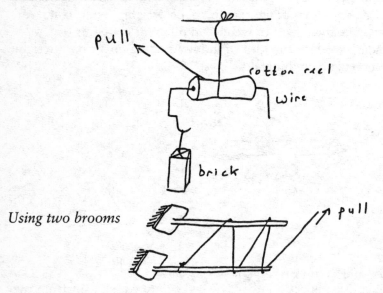

pull
cotton reel
wire
brick

Using two brooms
pull

Tie some string round two brooms and get two people to hold them steady while another pulls the string. It is impossible to keep the brooms apart because the presence of the string gives great advantage in strength over the two people holding the brooms.

Overcoming gravity

By placing a ruler across a pencil and balancing a coin on one end you can overcome the downward pull of gravity if you drop another coin on the opposite end of the ruler. This will make the first coin shoot up in the air. Similarly, an elephant on a see-saw would cause a person to shoot up in the air at the other end.

More speed, more force

You can deliver a large blow with a hammer by forcing it down as it is moving, making it fall faster than it would under gravity alone. The faster your blows the quicker the nail goes in.

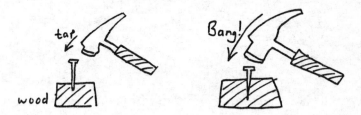

Fuels

Your child should be aware of the variety of fuels used in the home and in industry: coal, wood, oil and gas.

Micro-electronic devices

These include the computer chip, radio transistor, amplifier components etc. Explain to your child the wide occurrence of such components in the modern world and find some relevant books for him in the library.

Solubility
Get your child to try dissolving sugar and flour in water and compare the results.

Crystals Dissolve as much salt in warm water as possible, and let it cool. Leave the solution for a day or more and the crystals will grow.

Reproduction
Your child should know that all life is reproduced and that the 'adult' has 'babies' of a sort – such as kittens, puppies, lambs, ducklings, chicks, tadpoles.

Children should be able to see the hatching of eggs, either from frogspawn or a hen's egg, at some time. Explain that the cockerel or male is necessary for fertilisation.

Plants A good reference book will help discussion here. Talk about how flowers produce *pollen* which is carried by wind, insects or other means to different flowers where it helps to form *seeds*. These are sometimes found in *fruits* and can make new plants:

acorn
makes a new oak tree

eaten by birds
holly leaf

Point out that some seeds are found in plants. Here are a few examples.
Fruits tomato, apple, pear, orange, lemon, raspberry, blackberry
Nuts are seeds: coconut, walnut, almond, peanut
Cones

Health and the environment Your child should be aware of environmental pollution and the dangers to health caused by car fumes, factory smoke, poisons in rivers and the sea, asbestos, cigarette smoking, nuclear radiation, too much sunlight, and X-rays.

There are small amounts of poisonous substances in the water we drink and the food we eat – fish may take in poison from the sea or river water, fruit may have been sprayed with chemicals, and meat may contain certain additives.

Some foods are better for us than others. Explain that too much fat is bad for us as it helps to block up the arteries that supply the heart and thus cause a heart attack. In order to keep the body in good working order we need minerals and vitamins from fruit and vegetables. Point out that sweets decay teeth and have no value as a food. When foods 'go off' (*decay*) they contain dangerous germs. Flies also carry dangerous germs and can contaminate food. We should keep food cool in the fridge so that 'germs' will not multiply in a warm atmosphere causing food to deteriorate. (*See* also page 62.)

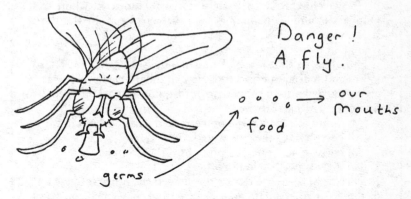

Viruses are also 'germs' and can feed, grow and reproduce. Many viruses are harmless to humans whilst others cause childhood diseases such as: colds, flu, chicken-pox, mumps, measles, German measles. Today vaccination can prevent some of these.

GRADED TESTS
FOR 9 TO 11 YEAR OLDS
ENGLISH

TEST 1

(1) COMPREHENSION

Quickly Joseph fished for the ring of keys and hauled it up. A few minutes later he was kneeling beside the senseless body, hastily stripping off the uniform. There was no time to lose. Already the locking up of the prisoners had started and he could hear the guards shouting at them outside.

Joseph felt warm in the guard's uniform. The great coat reached to his ankles. The fur coat had flaps for covering his ears. He smiled to himself as he locked the guard in the freezing cell. Then, turning up his collar so that the tips touched his cheek bones, he went out into the bitter night.

He walked through the snow towards Block E, where the Hungarian and Romanian prisoners were kept. In the dark shadows behind the huts he hid until the trumpet sounded the change of guard.

Hundreds of times he had watched the soldiers of the guard fall in and march out of camp. He had memorised every order, every movement. It seemed to him quite natural now to be lining up with the others.

'Anything to report?' the officer asked each of them in turn.

'All correct, sir,' they answered.

'All correct, sir,' said Joseph in his best German.

'Guard, dismiss!' said the officer.

Joseph dropped to the rear and followed the other soldiers out of the great spiked gate and into freedom. It seemed too good to be true.

From *The Silver Sword* by Ian Serraillier

Questions

(a)   Why did Joseph smile to himself?

(b)   What prisoners were kept in Block E?

(c)   What had Joseph memorised?

(d)   What nationality are the guards?

(e)   Why did Joseph feel 'It seemed too good to be true'?

(f)   Why did Joseph hide in the dark shadows?

(2) Write down the opposites to these words and make sentences from them:

absence, answer, backward, beautiful, bright, cheap, difficult, divide, early, empty, enemy, entrance, evening, everywhere, failure, few, guilty, honest, ignorant, inferior, junior.

TEST 2

(1) Give words similar in meaning to these and make sentences from them:

abandon, abundant, commence, conversation,

difficult, leave, conceal, glance, imitate,

maximum, modern, moisture.

(2) Fit these words into the right place in the sentences:

(a) He .... me in the ....
     (missed, mist).

(b) 'I'm not .... to speak .... '
     (allowed, aloud).

(c) He jumped from the .... of the boat to the
     .... of the tree (bough, bow).

(d) 'Can you .... that you have written the
     .... correctly?' (cheque, check).

(e) We ate our .... and watched the
     .... on television (cereal, serial).

(f) It was some time .... that we
     .... the house (passed, past).

(3) Put these in the *past* tense:

(a) He is very happy.

(b) I drive to town.

(c) I ring the bell.

(d) I bite the apple.

(e) I know nothing.

(f) I speak Italian.

(g) He chooses the book.

(h) They eat the dinner.

(i) He falls down.

(j) He goes to the shop.

(k) He writes the letter.

TEST 3

(1) Write down the opposites of these words and make sentences from them:

loud, love, reveal, nowhere, numerous, peace, smart, smooth, soft, stationary, straight, temporary, transparent, truth, vacant.

(2) Put these sentences in the right order:

The teacher sent a note home.

The class chose the zoo trip.

They hired a bus.

The teacher said there would be a school trip.

Next day they went to the zoo.

She asked them to choose where they should go.

The teacher collected the money.

(3) Put these words in order:

(a) Tomorrow raining lovely today is day but could be it a

(b) Shall go to I want if nobody stop will me want and

(4) Write similar words to these and put them into sentences:

odour, peculiar, prohibit, powerful, purchase, ramble, rapid, reveal, stern, suspended, unite, vacant, wealth.

TEST 4

(1) COMPREHENSION

William pretends to be on a desert island

At last they turned towards the hut. 'We must find something to eat,' said William firmly. 'We can't let ourselves starve to death.'

'Shrimps?' suggested Peggy, cheerfully.

'We haven't got nets,' said William. 'We couldn't save them from the wreck.'

'Periwinkles?'

'There aren't any on this island. I know! Seaweed! An' we'll cook it.'

'Oh, how lovely!'

He gathered up a handful of seaweed and they entered the

hut, leaving a white handkerchief tied to the door to attract the attention of any passing ship. The hut was provided with a gas ring and William, disregarding his family's express injunction, lit this and put on a saucepan filled with water and seaweed.

'We'll pretend it's a wood fire,' he said. 'We couldn't make a real wood fire out on the prom. They'd stop us. So we'll pretend this is. An' we'll pretend we saved a saucepan from the wreck.'

After a few minutes he took off the pan and drew out a long green strand.

'You eat it first,' he said politely.

The smell of it was not pleasant. Peggy drew back.

'Oh, no, you first!'

'No, you,' said William nobly. 'You look hungrier than me.'

She bit off a piece, chewed it, shut her eyes and swallowed.

'Now you,' she said with a shade of vindictiveness in her voice. 'You're not going to not have any.'

William took a mouthful and shivered.

'I think it's gone bad,' he said critically.

Peggy's rosy face had paled.

'I'm going home,' she said suddenly.

'You can't go home on a desert island,' said William severely.

'Well, I'm going to be rescued then,' she said.

'I think I am, too,' said William.

From *William and the Smuggler* by Richmal Crompton

Questions

(a)   Why does William tie a handkerchief to the hut door?

(b)   What do the two cook to eat?

(c)   Why does William try to get Peggy to eat it first?

(d)   Why did Peggy close her eyes to swallow?

(e)   Why did William shiver?

(f)   What made Peggy decide to 'go home'?

(g)   Why did William say, 'You can't go home'?

(h)   Peggy said she was going to be 'rescued then'. Why does this make more sense than just going home?

(2)   Correct these sentences.

    (a)   I am the oldest of the two.

    (b)   Neither dad or mum was there.

    (c)   He is not as old as me.

    (d)   The film what we watched was interesting.

(e) I cannot eat no more.

(f) I have forgot what the time is.

(g) She hurted herself.

(3) Punctuate, put in capitals and correct the spelling in the following:

deer liverpool manager,

   i am ritin to inform yu that i am a yung footborler hoo lives in london i fink yore teem is brillyant but so am i i scored the only gowl up the park today agaynst mi frend filip stocks he even sed to me cor benny that was brillyant it was at leest as good as eny fink in the world cup an uvver tyme i neerly scored a gowl and filip tripedme up i sed thats a penaltee and he sed no its not and i sed yore a cheet and he sed yu stink enyway so we arnt frends enymor but i am stil a brilyunt footborler praps yu wood lyke to put me on tryal i wood reely lyke to play for liverpool then i cood be famous an not go to skool enymor

yores

Benny

TEST 5

(1) COMPREHENSION

How to recognise a Witch

'What other things must I look for to recognise a witch?' I asked.

'Look for the nose-holes,' my grandmother said. 'Witches have slightly larger nose-holes than ordinary people. The rim of each nose-hole is pink and curvy, like the rim of a certain kind of sea-shell.'

'Why do they have such big nose-holes?' I asked.

'For smelling with,' my grandmother said. 'A REAL WITCH has the most amazing powers of smell. She can actually smell out a child who is standing on the other side of the street on a pitch-black night.'

'She couldn't smell me,' I said. 'I've just had a bath.'

'Oh yes, she could,' my grandmother said. 'The cleaner you happen to be, the more smelly you are to a witch.'

'That can't be true,' I said.

'An absolutely clean child gives off the most ghastly smell to a witch,' my grandmother said. 'The dirtier you are, the less you smell.'

'But that doesn't make sense, Grandma.'

'Oh yes, it does,' my grandmother said.

'It isn't the *dirt* that the witch is smelling. It is *you*. The smell that drives a witch mad comes right out of your own skin. It comes oozing out of your skin in waves, and these waves, stink-waves the witches call them, go floating through the air and hit the witch right smack in her nostrils. They send her reeling.'

From *The Witches* by Roald Dahl

Questions

(a) What is special about witches?

(b) Why does it not help to have a bath?

(c) What sends a witch reeling?

(d) Why does the boy say, 'But that doesn't make sense, Grandma.'?

(e) How does Grandma make sense of this nonsense?

(f) Why do you think that the boy is so keen to know about witches?

(g) Explain these words:
ghastly, pitch-black, oozing, stench, absolutely, nostrils.

(2) Add at least five more words to make sentences of the following:

(a) I saw the boy ....

(b) I noticed ....

(c) He saved ....

(d) The train came rushing ....

(e) The man looked suspicious ....

(f) I know the girl ....

(g) The man shouted and waved frantically ....

(3) Add at least five words at the beginning to make sentences of the following:

(a) .... I could not swim.

(b) .... was caught by the police.

(c) .... was as tall as a tree.

(d) .... cannot swim.

(e) .... slipped on a banana skin.

(f) .... by mistakes.

MATHEMATICS

TEST 1

(1)   712
     − 176
     _____

(2)   842
     − 376
     _____

(3)   900
     − 185
     _____

(4)   126
     ×   3
     _____

(5)   237
     ×   4
     _____

(6)   569
     ×   4
     _____

(7) 3) 27

(8) 3) 51

(9) 4) 72

(10) 2) 334

(11)

(a) $\dfrac{1}{2} = \dfrac{}{8}$

(b) $\dfrac{1}{4} = \dfrac{}{8}$

(c) $\dfrac{3}{4} = \dfrac{}{8}$

(d) $\dfrac{1}{4} + \dfrac{1}{4} = \dfrac{}{4}$

(e) $\dfrac{1}{2} + \dfrac{1}{4} = \dfrac{}{4}$

(f) $\dfrac{1}{8} + \dfrac{1}{8} = \dfrac{}{4}$

(g) $\dfrac{1}{4} + \dfrac{2}{8} = \dfrac{}{4} = \dfrac{}{2}$

(h) $\dfrac{1}{2} + \dfrac{2}{8} = \dfrac{}{4}$

TEST 2

(1)   132
     ×   6
     _____

(2)   234
     ×   7
     _____

(3)   352
     ×   8
     _____

(4)   Using the 100 equivalence diagram, change to decimals:

(a) $\dfrac{1}{10}$

(b) $\dfrac{1}{100}$

(c) $\dfrac{3}{100}$

(d) $\dfrac{5}{100}$ (e) $\dfrac{10}{100}$ (f) $\dfrac{15}{100}$

(g) $\dfrac{11}{10}$ (h) $2\dfrac{1}{100}$

(5) Change to fractions:

    (a) 0.1 (b) 0.03 (c) 0.4

    (d) 0.10 (e) 0.15 (f) 1.2

    (g) 2.03

(6) Find $\dfrac{1}{10}$ of 1 metre in centimetres.

(7) What is $\dfrac{3}{10}$ of 1 metre?

(8) What is $\dfrac{1}{10}$ of 50?

TEST 3

(1) $\begin{array}{r} 372 \\ \times\quad 8 \\ \hline \\ \hline \end{array}$ (2) $\begin{array}{r} 416 \\ \times\quad 9 \\ \hline \\ \hline \end{array}$ (3) $6\,)\,\overline{\,84\,}$

(4) $7\,)\,\overline{\,84\,}$ (5) $8\,)\,\overline{\,96\,}$ (6) $9\,)\,\overline{\,108\,}$

(7) What is $\dfrac{1}{4}$ of 20? ....   (8) What is $\dfrac{3}{4}$ of 20?...........

(9) A father is three times as old as his son. How old is the son if the father is 36? ....

(10) What are these times in 24-hour-clock time?

    (a) 11.30 am...................... (b) 1.00 pm ....

    (c) 2.00 pm........................ (d) 7.00 pm ....

(11) How long is it from 2.00 pm to 5.30 pm? ....

(12) How long is it from 10.30 am to 4.00 pm?........................

(13) How long is it from 11.00 pm on Monday to 6.30 am the next day? ....

(14) What is $\dfrac{1}{4}$ of £2.00? ....

(15) What is $\dfrac{3}{4}$ of £2.00? ....

TEST 4

(1)   376
    ×   7
    ‾‾‾‾‾‾

(2) 2) 972   (3) 3) 1044

(4) Bus Timetable

TOWN	BUS 1	BUS 2	BUS 3
Alford	11.35	12.40	16.20
Bilton	13.20	14.15	18.02

(a) Which bus is the quickest? ....
     How long does it take? ....

(b) If a man gets to Bilton on the 11.35 Alford bus, how
     long does he have to wait for the next bus? ....

(5) What shape does this make? ....

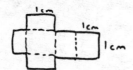

(6) What shape does this net make? ....

(7)

```
5 ┌─┬─┬─┬─┬─┬─┐
4 ├─┼─┼─┼─┼─┼─┤
3 ├─┼─┼─┼─┼─┼─┤
2 ├─┼─┼─┼─┼─┼─┤
1 ├─┼─┼─┼─┼─┼─┤
0 └─┴─┴─┴─┴─┴─┘
  0 1 2 3 4 5 6
```

Mark these points on the above:
(2,3)   (4,1)   (0,2)
(2,0)   (0,0)   (6,5)

(8) What is $\frac{1}{4}$ of 1 kg? ....

(9) What is $\frac{3}{4}$ of 1 kg? ....

(10) Are these angles *acute*, *obtuse*, or *reflex*?

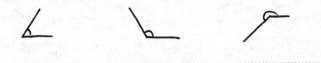

....

(11) If you turn clockwise from E to N, how many degrees do
      you turn through? ....

(12) What is the chance of getting a 'heads'
      if I throw a coin? ....

(13) What is the chance of getting an *even* number
      if I throw a dice? ....

TEST 5

(1) $\begin{array}{r} 347 \\ \times\ \ \ 9 \\ \hline \\ \hline \end{array}$

(2) $8\overline{)\ 7\ 9\ 1}$

(3) $\frac{1}{6} + \frac{1}{12} =$ ....

(4) $\frac{1}{2} + \frac{1}{8} =$ ....

(5) $1\frac{1}{10} + 2\frac{3}{10} =$ ....

(6) $\frac{2}{5} + \frac{3}{10} =$ ....

(7) $\frac{2}{3} + \frac{1}{9} =$ ....

(8) What are these the *nets* of? ....

(a)   (b)

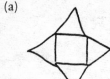   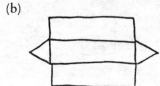

(9) On the clock how many degrees are there between the o'clock and 25 past the hour? ....

(10) 23 × 10 = ... (11) 23 × 100 = ...

(12) 400 ÷ 10 = ... (13) 400 ÷ 100 = ...

(14) What line is perpendicular to the E–W line? ....

(a) door   (b) floor   (c) television

(d) a wall   (e) a window

(15) Which of these objects are in the horizontal plane?

....

Which are vertical? ....

(16) Trace the picture below. Then place your pencil on the X and turn through 90° and 180° (centre is the centre of the X). The image will be rotated through the angles.

x

TEST 6

(1)   £
          7.00
        − 1.93
        _____

        _____

(2) Add £1.24, £0.39 and 3p ....

(3) What is the mean of these numbers? ....

3,   4,   7,   6,   1,   7,   7

(4)   £   (5)   £
        0.45   1.23
    ×   3   ×   6
    ─────   ─────

    ─────   ─────

(6) I buy 7 books at £1.56 each.
     What is my change from £15.00? ....

(7) Say whether there is *no chance*, a *half chance*, or a
     certainty in the following examples:

     (a) that I will never be born ....

     (b) that I will throw a 'tail' of a coin ....

     (c) that numbers 1 to 6 will occur when I throw a
          normal dice? ....

(8) Use the number line and tick if these are correct.

     (a) 4 > 1   (b) 2 < 3   ┬ +4
                                                          ├ +3
     (c) 3 > 3   (d) −0 > −2   ├ +2
                                                          ├ +1
     (e) 2 > −3   (f) −1 > −6?   ┼ 0
                                                          ├ −1
(9) How many 500 g are there in 1 kg? ....   ├ −2
                                                          ├ −3
(10) How many 250 g are there in 1 kg? ....   ├ −4
                                                          ├ −5
(11) How many books costing £2.50 can I buy   ┴ −6
     for £10.00? ....

(12) $\frac{1}{2}$ km = ... m

(13) $\frac{1}{4}$ km = ... m

(14) $\frac{3}{4}$ km = ... m

(15) 1 mm = ... cm

(16) 12 mm = ... cm

(17) 150 cm = ... m

(18) 2000 g = ... kg

TEST 7

(1) $\frac{1}{2} + \frac{1}{3}$ = ...   (3) $2\frac{1}{4}$ = $\frac{}{4}$

(2) $\frac{1}{4} + \frac{1}{3}$ = ...   (4) $3\frac{2}{5}$ = $\frac{}{5}$

(5) $1\frac{1}{2} + 1\frac{1}{4}$ = ...

(6) 0.80 m = ... cm

(7) 0.800 km = ... m

(8) 0.4 cm = ... mm

(9) 0.40 m = ... cm

(10) What must be added to one-half to make two-thirds? ....

(11) $\frac{1}{6}$ of 18p = ... p

(12) $\frac{5}{6}$ of 18p = ... p

(13) How many thirds in 1 whole? ....

(14) How many thirds in 4 whole ones? ....

(15)

	mins	secs
	2	24
+	1	35

(16)

	hours	mins
	3	20
−	1	40

(17) Throw two dice. You may get 1 with 2, or 6 with 3. Write these as 1,2 and 6,3 and complete the table showing all the possible number pairs you can get:

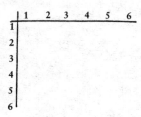

(18) (a) How many 1 cm cubes can be fitted into a box which is 2 cm high, 3 cm long and 2 cm wide?

....

(b) How many cubes have only *two* faces showing?

....

 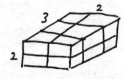

(19) If a boy has more than or equal to 20p for pocket money, he puts 5p in his money box and spends the rest of it. If he has less than 20p he spends it. If he has more than 50p, he puts it all in his bank account. Finish the diagram:

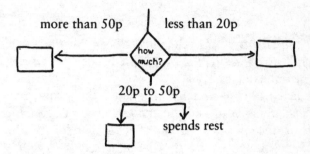

(Answers to the questions in these Graded Mathematics tests can be found on page 183.)

CONCLUSION

(1) Learn from your child, how he or she *thinks*. Help your child to *visualise* a sum, problem, ideas in stories or word meanings.

(2) Leave *time*, especially where Maths problems are concerned, for your child to try various strategies.

(3) Learning periods should be in a relaxed atmosphere. Humour helps relaxation. The length of learning periods should be tailored to the age of your child.

(4) Motivation should be secured by suggesting both short-term and long-term rewards (parental approval, a break to look forward to, an exam in the future, etc.).

(5) Material should be presented as clearly as possible so that your child can create a clear mental image to 'match' with memory.

(6) Practice is vital, although it should never become drudgery. Learning by rote should be mixed with the practice of work that promotes understanding.

(7) Meaning in a deep sense is important, and reference back to real life should occur frequently, *whatever* the age of the child.

We think, and learn, in *meanings*, and where incoming messages link with memory it is through mental images which confer various levels of meaning to the information. The level of meaning depends on concentration, or on the presence or absence of material in memory. The development of skills is important, and the establishing of networks in memory built on skills should not be underestimated (for example, knowledge of tables and sums learnt as processes). However, you should also develop in your child's memory networks that represent deeper meanings. In school and in life, ultimately, these will be more valuable and also help a child to feel confident when faced with a wide variety of problems both academically and in the outside world.

THE NATIONAL CURRICULUM

Important attainments for Mathematics
Age 7 Approximately level 2. 'Bright' go to level 3.
Age 11 Approximately level 4 (some into level 5).
(*Note* Some *number* targets are far exceeded by many preparatory schools).

Level 1 Numbers up to 10; counting, reading writing and ordering. Addition, subtraction up to 10 (real objects).
Estimating number of objects up to 10.
Sorting 2-D and 3-D shapes.
Drawing 2-D shapes. Mapping diagrams. Repeating patterns.

Level 2 Numbers up to 100. Tens and Units.
Adding, subtracting up to 10.
'difference'. Money in adding and subtracting.
Estimating number of objects up to 20.
Patterns in addition and subtraction up to 10.
Odd/Even. Symbol for a number.
Recognising shapes: square, rectangle, circle, triangle, hexagon, pentagon, cube, cuboid, cylinder, sphere.
Notion of angle.
Notion of translation, rotation, reflection.
Frequency tables, block graphs.

Level 3 Numbers to 1000. Place value.
Decimal notation for money.
Temperature scale: negative numbers.
+ and − to 20 (include zero).
× and ÷
2×, 5× and 10× tables. Approximate to the nearest 10 or 100.
Remainders. Round up or down.
Function machines.
Reflective symmetry in 2-D and 3-D shapes.
Measurement: length (km, cm), weight (kg, g), volume (litre, ml or cm)
Interpretation of bar charts and pictograms where the symbol represents a group of units: e.g.   = 20,   = under 20/
Chance: 'Likelihood', 'Evens', 'fair', 'unfair'.

Level 4 ×10 and ×100.
Decimals to 2 D.P. + and −
Place values. Simple fractions. Percentages.
Tables to 10×
+ and − (3-digit). × and ÷ (2-digit)
Problems: 2-digit decimals, × and ÷ with whole numbers.
Equivalence of fractions.

Function machine (e.g. ×2+1)
And, 2 × 7 = 14, 14 ÷ 7 = 2 (inverse).
Co-ordinates. Grid on ordinance survey map.
Areas by counting squares. Volumes by counting cubes.
Estimation of range in everyday life.
Mean and range.
Decision Tree Diagrams.
Use of Times Tables.
Estimate length, height, capacity, weight.
Acute angle, obtuse angle, reflex angle, perpendicular, vertical, horizontal.
Nets for cubes, pyramids, prisms.
Rotation using tracing paper.

Chance:	0		1.0
	no	Evens	Certainty
	chance		1

Important attainment targets for English
Level 1 Recognise own name. Recognise 'bus-stop', 'Exit', 'Danger'. Begin to recognise individual words or letters.
Use of pictures, symbols, isolated letters.
Difference between letters and numbers.
Write letter shapes in response to sounds.
Use single letters or letter groups to represent whole words.
Copying letters.

Level 2 Read labels on drawers and simple menus.
Knowledge of the alphabet.
Phonics.
Read a range of material.
Talk about a story.
Independent pieces of writing using complete sentences.
Capital letters, full stops, question marks.
Write stories with an opening and more than one character.
Other, simple writing.
Spell a range of common words including those *they* use commonly.
Recognise spelling patterns.
Produce capital and lower case letter.

Level 3 Relate verbally a story with a beginning, middle and end; to recount a series of incidents at home or in science.
Expression in reading.
Silent reading.
Discussion about the way stories are structured.
Use of reference books for projects, etc.
Writing with complete sentences, capital letters and full stops or question marks, with more connections than 'and' and 'then'.
Correct use of tense and pronouns.
Recognise common letter strings (-ion, -ing, -ous).
Word family awareness.
Checking spelling.
Joined-up writing.

Level 4 Detailed oral accounts.
Extending the use of library, including the catalogue system.
Accurate punctuation.
Interesting stories.
Investigation accounts.
Writing extended to letters, poems, invitations, posters, etc.
Knowledge for spelling of the main prefixes and suffixes.

ANSWERS

Answers to Graded Mathematics Tests for 9 to 11 year olds

TEST 1: (1) 536   (2) 466   (3) 715   (4) 378   (5) 948   (6) 2276   (7) 9   (8) 17   (9) 18
(10) 167   (11) (a) $\frac{4}{8}$ (b) $\frac{2}{8}$ (c) $\frac{6}{8}$ (d) $\frac{2}{4}$ (e) $\frac{3}{4}$ (f) $\frac{1}{4}$ (g) $\frac{2}{4} = \frac{1}{2}$ (h) $\frac{3}{4}$

TEST 2: (1) 792   (2) 1638   (3) 2816   (4) (a) 0.1 (b) 0.01 (c) 0.03 (d) 0.05 (e) 0.1
(f) 0.15 (g) 0.1 (h) 2.01   (5) (a) $\frac{1}{10}$ (b) $\frac{3}{100}$ (c) $\frac{4}{10}$ (d) $\frac{1}{10}$ (e) $\frac{15}{100}$ (f) $1\frac{2}{10}$ (g) $2\frac{3}{100}$ (6) 10 cm
(7) 30 cm   (8) 5

TEST 3: (1) 2976   (2) 3744   (3) 14 (4) 12   (5) 12   (6) 12   (7) 5   (8) 15   (9) 12
(10) (a) 11.30 (b) 13.00 (c) 14.00 (d) 19.00   (11) 3 hours 30 minutes   (12) 5 hours 30
minutes (13) 7 hours 30 minutes   (14) 50p   (15) £1.50

TEST 4: (1) 2632   (2) 486   (3) 348   (4) (a) Bus 2; 1 hour 35 minutes (b) Until 14.15;
55 minutes   (5) Cube   (6) Tetrahedron   (7) No answer required   (8) 250 g   (9) 750 g
(10) acute, obtuse, reflex   (11) 270°   (12) 1 in 2   (13) 1 in 2 (or 3 in 6)

TEST 5: (1) 3123   (2) 98 remainder 7 or $98\frac{7}{8}$ (3) $\frac{3}{12}$ or $\frac{1}{4}$ (4) $\frac{5}{8}$ (5) $3\frac{4}{10}$ (6) $\frac{7}{10}$ (7) $\frac{7}{9}$
(8) (a) square-based pyramid (b) prism   (9) 150°   (10) 230   (11) 2300   (12) 40   (13) 4
(14) N–S line   (15) (a) vertical (b) horizontal (c) horizontal (d) vertical (e) vertical
(16) No answer required

TEST 6: (1) £5.07   (2) £1.66   (3) 5   (4) £1.35   (5) £7.38   (6) £4.08   (7) (a) no chance
(b) half-chance (c) certainty   (8) (a) yes (b) yes (c) no (d) yes (e) yes (f) yes   (9) 2
(10) 4   (11) 4   (12) 500 m   (13) 250 m   (14) 750 m   (15) 0.1 cm   (16) 1.2 cm
(17) 1.5 cm   (18) 2 kg

TEST 7: (1) $\frac{5}{6}$ (2) $\frac{7}{12}$ (3) $\frac{9}{4}$ (4) $\frac{17}{5}$ (5) $2\frac{3}{4}$ (6) 80 cm   (7) 800 m   (8) 4 mm   (9) 40 cm
(10) $\frac{1}{6}$ (11) 3p   (12) 15p   (13) 3   (14) 12   (15) 3 minutes 59 seconds   (16) 1 hour 40
minutes (17) No answer required   (18) (a) 12 (b) 4   (19) No answer required

INDEX